#105
AILING, HEALING

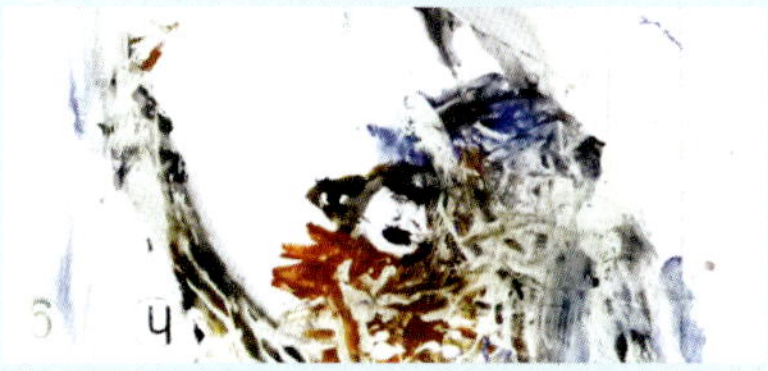

SEE

REGULARS

ESSAYS

POETRY

COVER: HIROKI GODENGI

105

AUTUMN 2014

WWW.NEWWELSHREVIEW.COM

New Welsh Review
PO Box 170, Aberystwyth, SY23 1WZ
Telephone: 01970 628410

ISBN: 9780957514171
ISSN: 09542116

New Welsh Review *is published with the financial support of the Welsh Books Council and Aberystwyth University.* New Welsh Review *was established in 1988 by Academi (now Literature Wales) and the Association for Welsh Writing in English.* New Welsh Review *also works in partnership with Wales Literature Exchange.*

Mae croeso ichi ohebu â'r golygydd yn Gymraeg.

SEE

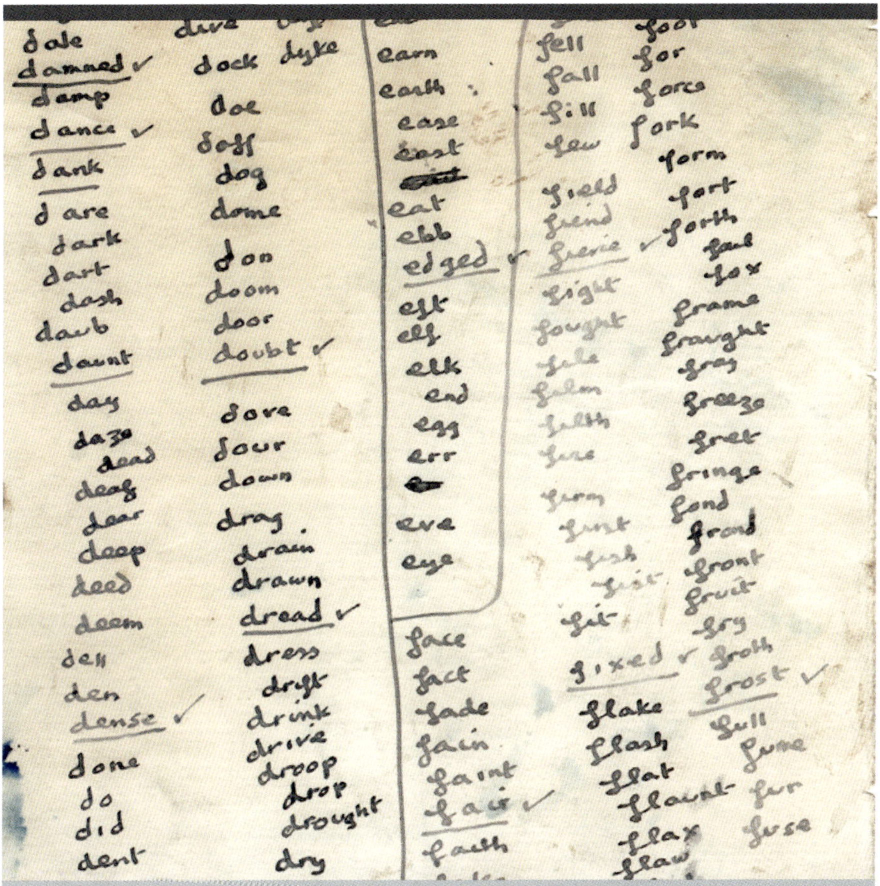

IMAGE: DYLAN THOMAS' WORDLIST, COURTESY DAVID HIGHAM ASSOCIATES ON BEHALF OF THE TRUSTEES FOR THE COPYRIGHT

DYLAN THOMAS' MANUSCRIPTS EXHIBITION

Dylan Thomas Centre, Swansea
dylanthomas.com
5 September – 24 December

Comprises manuscripts of poems, a list of rhyming words and a series of black and white photographs of Dylan Thomas, many of which have not been widely displayed or reproduced. Items are on loan from the University of Buffalo.

EDITOR¶

GWEN DAVIES

LIFE IS SWEET, AND SHORT

• THIS ISSUE, SUBTITLED *AILING, HEALING*, LOOKS AT ART, ILLNESS AND healing. Travel writers Gwyneth Lewis and John Harrison talked to me at Hay this year on the subject, including the balming boundaries of seamanship; the Bosun's chimp as the barometer of a marriage's health; the soothing heartbeat of iambic pentameter; being put on a hospital's E-bay, and colonizing cancer as Conquistadors.

• More on the theme: Michael Nath dices with death on p7; Jane MacNamee learns to walk again following surgery (p51); a boy's death mends a marriage in Candy Neubert's story on p35; Ellie Rees comes to terms with her son's paralysis, on p31; trangressional sex and literature help a grieving widow in Michael Nott's review of Andrés Neuman's novel, *Talking to Ourselves* (p84) while Dr Iwan has OCD in Ellen Bell's review of graphic novel, *The Bad Doctor*. Meanwhile, Swansea-Iraqi comedian Nadia Kamil's profile of Judith Owen reveals a shared experience of losing a mother young, and Judith's depression, which led her to co-host and score 'Losing It', Ruby Wax's stage show on mental illness (p14). STOPPRESS: We are sad to note the death of valued contributor, Charlotte Greig/Williams whose essay on Molly Drake was in NWR 103.

• Autumn videos are themed around Crime, Punishment & Enfranchisment, covering Wiliam Owen Roberts (on his European epic *Petrograd* in translation), Heini Gruffudd (on his Welsh-Jewish family memoir, *A Haven from Hitler*) and Diarmait Mac Giolla Chriost (prison literature in Welsh).

• Entries open until 1 November for New Welsh Writing Awards, celebrating short books and long-form essays on the environment! £1000 cash and e-pub deal for works between 8,000 and 30,000 words. See inside back cover.

• Micro-review of *Story*, Vol II (Library of Wales), ed Dai Smith: Too much politics (formal & informal); too industrial; too Sixties Generation; right to celebrate Leonora Brito, wrong to ignore Cynan Jones & Mary-Ann Constantine.

LIBRARY OF WALES

The very best of Welsh short fiction. Required reading for anyone from Edinburgh to Ely and from London to Llanfrothen...

Story: The Library of Wales short story anthology, Volume 1 — Edited by Dai Smith

Story: The Library of Wales short story anthology, Volume 2 — Edited by Dai Smith

www.thelibraryofwales.com

Join us on foreign shores...

From the 14th Century spice route to a coming of age in Ghana, and a mother's experience of suffering and salvation in Saudi Arabia.

The Storyteller's Granddaughter
MARGARET REDFERN
ISBN: 9781909983014

In a Foreign Country
Hilary Shepherd
ISBN: 9781906784621

'By turns gripping, provoking and vividly sensory'
Tiffany Atkinson

INSH ALLAH
Alys Einion
ISBN: 9781909983083

honno | www.honno.co.uk | facebook.com/honnopress | twitter.com/honno

EVERY LAUGH IS A DICE THROW

MICHAEL NATH DICES WITH DEATH

> **On the shelf was a stack of cardboard Trilbys, vessels for throwing up in. My wife was making calls like Napoleon.**

HOW LONG YOU HAD THAT COUGH?

Since I skated against the wind in Flanders.[1]

Seriously, you should get it checked out.

But you don't want it checked out, for a long cough can be a sign of you know what.

Though you have been giving thought to the issue....

On the great British cake show, an anamorphic skull. Like, the *vanity* of baking, and all worldly effort!

You are going to die. Tell a punter on Wind Street, you'll be slapped, or pinched – repeated three times, it's harassment.... Unless you're an oncologist or narcissist – or Big Joe Turner: 'You're so beautiful but you're gonna die someday.'

At a certain age, it comes into view. Wow, look at that! A mountain range. You thought you were just driving, like the younger folk behind, but there it is. Keep quiet. Don't spoil it for them.

There's always something to do before we get there. My grandmother wanted to see Brittany (she heard it was like the Gower). Jenks told me he was going to visit the most dangerous farm in Mexico, where killer chillies grow (one of those lads could take out Cardiff). He never made it either. Rita had herself a Richard Dawkins tattoo, against the dying of the light.

Time to plan your last meal.

I'll have a pound of liquorice hard-tack. By the time I've finished chewing, the guards will have gone off shift. And a bottle of Wray & Nephew. Get them pissed and pinch the keys.

Be serious for a minute. Martin Heidegger says you don't live true to yourself until you've imagined your own death as the thing that makes you unique. Ah. Though JP Sartre says the death you imagine isn't the one you get. When you think of your last meal, you forget the cancer will have made you so sick you can't stomach anything. They have to stick the morphine in your arse or you'll throw that up as well.

OK. I'll imagine cancer more factually. I'll go out and get a book on it.

Careful! Seen the weather out there? Owch! So much potential and he's copped it. Wasn't much older than Jim Morrison. Lifelong ambition to fight cancer with dignity. Sign outside the kebab shop, blew off and broke his neck.

When Dad died, I couldn't believe he was gone: but believe I must, for he wasn't in his chair or Merc. On check paper I tried to philosophise. Georges Bataille talks about negative miracles. Such was the death of my old man, perhaps: 'Impossible, but there you are.' But I was mistaken to be staring through a hole in the future cut in his shape. For when I looked back over the final months, matching dates with his death, so he had exactly seven months left, or five or four, I saw that under the aspect of the past, he was at those times immortal – life without death was guaranteed him. So in memory, I was beside a man who could not die that day, when we drove up in the snow to examine the bombers at Duxford and he showed me turbines like those he used to work on. We know death to be possible at any time, but only when we look ahead.

Eternity is behind us. Indelibly, you have been. You and you only, name, face, style of being. That was you. When you won that fight with a cross-eyed kid and they carried you on their shoulders. Walking to school in fog with lads from the estate, voices booming. Rita Jones – the time she kissed you at the fair. All behind you, but still there. How d'you feel about that, kiddo?

You want more, though? Like a man who can't get himself to bed in case he misses something? Put your head down now and remember. See what you can find unaided. In the morning, try the attic. Crates of letters, photos, seasons – what a life! So much stretching back, and not on your road only; your life passed into others' and they haven't forgotten. So many of you back there! Your you, and theirs.

Those certificates Mam let you have. John Howells, her grandfather: 'Mason at marriage (13 August, 1904). Coal hewer at death.' He built Nebo Chapel at Glyncorrwg. Wall on the right cut slant to fit the valley, elms above. Perhaps you're like him....

Plays change and masks, said Schopenhauer, the actors stay the same. Not that John H passed into you intact, but you repeat essential gestures: making a church no one goes to anymore; writing novels. The named self you cling to is the least of you. You are generally immortal. 'Moral cells' Proust called them, those habits and expressions which eternally appear in individuals of the same series. That way of laughing more than smiling, the liking for rum and beer, the manner of leaving a room – a witness would say the great-grandson's just the same. In fact the witnesses must be immortal too.

Two scenes are alike. Prince Hamlet among the graves: 'To what base uses we may return, Horatio!' You could bung a beer barrel with Alexander the Great, block a mouse hole with Caesar. Don Quixote at a Barcelona printing house, his life in a box of pages. All may be vanity, but just beyond is hilarity.

They pass away with friends to hand, issuing instructions. And such deaths go back to Socrates, bathing and chatting as the hemlock froze his legs, reminding Crito to make sacrifice; to King David, with a lass to warm his limbs as he fixes the succession.

Falstaff turned cold from the feet up. Socrates and David must have been in Shakespeare's mind. The old knight smiled and played with flowers, he sung a psalm. Made a fine end, says the Hostess, went away like a child. Not to hell, this old sinner, but to Wales; for he's gone to 'Arthur's bosom'. King David went 'the way of all the earth', with sound words to his son, but Falstaff went to Arthur. Perhaps the best end of all.

With Christ, the image of death strikes terror. We used to dwell on this for eternity's sake; now we just have the terror, frightening ourselves off life itself. Look at our regulations. 'Health and Safety' dominates us like a sky god. Flash photography can set off a bomb in your head. Disturbing images may destroy your comfort. Warn viewers. Warn them not to 'approach' this man under any circumstances in case they all flock to him like the kids of Hamelin. Round off the news with a severe weather warning. No one looks out the window anymore in case a hoodie stabs them with a toothpick on a pole. A sandwich box has more text than the Lord's Prayer. You go to work and it's security status 'Amber'. They make you leave early 'due to' snow/heat/wind. The announcer tells you not to slip. The announcer tells you to bring a bottle – not a bottle of tawny port, you berk, a bottle of Evian still. People walk the streets clutching water. They've got security console wristbands to measure humidity, radioactivity, whether there's a riot going on. For God's sake, this is Britain. There's hardly anything to die of.

That's what you think....

On Valentine's Day, here it came.... Are you acquainted with the edge of death? *Why, sir, 'tis a sort of grey struggling dream.* With cordial thumps the missus brought me back, howling in my eye. She's a top doctor herself, but resus isn't her scene.

Ta! I'll be off to work now.

You were blue as Stilton, you fool!

Enter paramedics with electrodes. So he was laughing at something then the cough took him down? The skipper was a good man with a Chelsea tattoo. In the ambulance they watched me like an IED. We entered A&E the back way. They asked if I knew the date. Thc nurse who wired me was highbrow. On the shelf was a stack of cardboard trilbys, vessels for throwing up in. My wife was making calls like Napoleon. The nurse chatted about *Ulysses* and Chaucer, eye on the monitors behind. A neurologist asked gently if I'd pissed myself. The word for today was 'syncope'. Enter an Italian with the scanner. Do you know how much an ex-smoker does *not* want a chest x-ray?

I really ought to vamoose. Got a class at eleven.

You're going nowhere, pal! sang this somber quartet. For dignity, they let me keep my shoes on. The door blew open like a dawn raid: medics bore a screaming women behind screens. She was going to die. The Italian was pointing at a screen over the way, like her gallery had just acquired a lost anatomy. Look at that, for Christ's sake! Look, everyone! Stop that woman screaming! Send postilions the length of the land! Tell them in Kiev!

Ever seen a pair of lungs so *clear*?

The woman screamed in stereo. In fact, she'd just given birth. The kid had lungs like mine. They should call it Michael bach.

They rolled me to the Acute Assessment Unit like a president who's been shot. We were four floors up, storm battering the rooftops. Fellas lay about in the manner of banqueting Romans. I had a cardboard demi-john to piss in. An Irish nurse came and took it away. It's a good-hearted world is the NHS. They did right to show it well in the Olympics. But all I wanted was out of there before they had me in pyjamas. I'd brought a novel by that cough-meister, Kafka. The hero visits the mansion of Mr 'Pollunder', and has trouble leaving. He gets roughed up by Pollunder's daughter. I knew how he felt. Bright-haired Hildegard had me in an armlock,[2] wanting blood. Two Greek lasses took over, listening for heart echo like they'd trapped a mugger. The Roman opposite was vague about the date; he wasn't too sure of the century (tip to dossers: how to get a free bed). A South Indian registrar sat with us. I humbly offered a diagnosis: whooping cough.

Ah, pertussis!

I loved this guy – he was nodding. The beauty of Pertussis is that it's not lung cancer, or COPD (in other words, not your *fault*); it has no other symptoms (for *fifty-five days* I'd been saying I feel fine); you don't have to stay the night. But here comes a soft-spoken specialist from Yorkshire and a mighty thighed Parisian consultant, to hear the chronicle of this cough, its span, changing sounds, productivity: so the sputum, Monsieur, what d'you say? Pond slime, Swarfega, gooseberry, limoncello? – Absinthe! Bravo! The marvellous thing about medicine is that doctors are much given to interpretation: they listen to the body like a difficult poem. One thing they're agreed on: with a condition like yours, every laugh is a dice throw.

In another bed, a Roman bawled for Librium; the wind sang like a hoover.

Michael Nath *teaches both Literature and Creative Writing at the University of Westminster. His latest novel is* British Story: A Romance *(Route, 2014); his previous novel,* La Rochelle *(Route, 2010), was shortlisted for the James Tait Black Memorial Prize for Fiction (2011). michaelnath.wordpress.com*

[1] Pinched from Laurence Sterne.

[2] The one known by Judo folk as *juji-gatame*.

WHO ARE THE WELSH KALE AND WHAT DO THEY SAY?

GEE WILLIAMS ON THE WELSH ROMA

'Who cannot be impressed by the Kale?'

HOW OFTEN DO YOU GET TO SOLVE A MYSTERY THAT'S LIVED WITH YOU FOR DECADES?

It began with truanting, me and Patsy, a pair of nine-year-olds in the golden age before parents could be texted. For the first time ever we were going to present ourselves to the ferryman and demand to be taken across the River Dee at Saltney. We made it to the jetty. When Mr Manifold's small wooden dinghy puttered up we scrambled in – as if on business – for a three-minute trip, rougher than expected.

This far bank was less populated even than home territory and in each direction vast flat fields of vegetables stretched with occasional lines of pickers. The sun grew intense and we grew bored. Finally we dawdled back to the ferry point discovering on the way that we both had mud-coloured potato prints of buttocks on our cotton dresses. A cat lay on the empty concrete steps with the boat tied up next to it. Mr Manifold had disappeared. 'Bugger!' Patsy said.

Only Ferry Lane, visible between overgrown hedges, was left to explore. The lane was featureless at first, then punctuated by field gates. It was beside one of these, half-concealed in a thicket of elder, that we came across the woman and her gypsy wagon. Empty shafts poked almost onto the tarmac... no horse. Such things are always described as 'colourful'. Hers was green, and shabbiness completed the camouflage effect. Despite the heat, she had a fire going which she tended from an ordinary kitchen stool – but by now we had stopped in amazement. We were used to seasonal travellers appearing in modern caravans pulled by trucks. Door to door they gave away peg dolls in return for scrap metal. But we had never seen a Romany. She was *old*. Her silver plait was threaded with black and her skirt was figured by hand stitching. Her face was lined and tanned to brown paper. Come to a sudden stop in front of her, two guilty girls giggled and were silent. We were looked up and down: she knew we were illicit, out of place. She said… something. And here's the rub. I know what I heard and I *almost* understood.

The history of the Welsh Roma (or Kale) is secret and fascinating. Yet their integrity is provable only now that this small ethnic pocket is threatened. First linguistically: in the seventeenth century, celebrated Gypsy King Abram Woods, subject of the 2009 animated film, *The Travelling Harpists*, was head of the foremost Romany family in Wales. It was through his line their specific dialect was preserved, enabling the Irish linguist John Sampson to produce *The Dialect of the Gypsies of Wales* in 1926. There may be no native speakers left now. But with the help of Manfri, Howell and Jim Woods of Bala, the last fluent users of Welsh Romany, Sampson produced a grammar and vocabulary of an inflected language with ancient roots traceable back to Sanskit. Two thousand years before Christ, the Vedic Indians had a word for knee: *nalaka*. In the vocabulary of the Wood family *and nowhere else* it was preserved as 'naj,' a unique retention, the sort of thing that drives philologists wild. And, while being settled and absorbed into the host population, the Woods continued in their cultural gifts. Eldra Jarman, née Roberts, (1917–2000), a great-granddaughter, was both a harpist herself, a scholar and proud of her Roma heritage. She wrote, with her husband Prof AOH Jarman of Cardiff University, *Y Sipsiwn Cymreig* detailing the Gypsy King's lineage.

Then comes DNA evidence, unavailable to Sampson. A darker side to the Kale history, it shows the outcome of social deprivation. A 1977 study of blood types included a consensual profiling[1] of a group of south Wales families. This gave the incidence of a particular gene in the general British population as 30–40%, in the modern Indian subcontinent population as 10-25% and in these Romany families as *7–23%*. By some strange trick of biochemistry, the Welsh Kale were more Indian than many Indians (a scientific finding that opens for critique the cruder misconceptions of race.) It also uncovered a source of real distress. This small number of families had – how much through choice and how much through harassment and exclusion? – remained a closed, itinerant community. The price paid was poor health and a raised level of recessive gene disorders. Yet again, researchers' records of the cooperative nature of their subjects is a rebuttal to the casual stereotyping meted out to travellers. The habitual tension between the wanderer and the settled continues, but who cannot be impressed by the Kale? They have preserved their uniqueness over four thousand years and four thousand miles.

The mystery remained of what was said to two truanting girls by a figure that even then seemed to have stepped out of her own past. Speakers of generic Romany suggested various possibilities to me along the lines of *Kushto divus gudlo chavalin* (Good day, nice children). It *was* along those lines but remember that English was our first language, our native one only being learned at school, and neither of us were adept Welsh speakers. As my Welsh was added to over years, so were pieces of the puzzle. Because this trilingual member of the Kale was speaking in Welsh. *Croeso* came quickly and it remains my only certainty. We were welcome at her fire. The rest? *Difyrion!* I think: we were amusements in her solitary afternoon. *Gylfinirod ar chwâl* is what I *believe* she said. She recognised a pair of little loose beaks (or skiving curlews) before they flew off.

Two of ***Gee Williams**' short fiction collections have been shortlisted for the Wales Book of the Year award and her novel,* Salvage *(Alcemi), won the Gold Fiction Award polled by readers and was shortlisted for the James Tait Black Memorial Prize for Fiction at Edinburgh Book Festival in 2008. Her literary thriller,* Desire Lines, *set in north Wales, will be published by Parthian in 2015.*

[1] PR Harper, EM Williams and E Sunderland in *Journal of Medical Genetics* (June, 1977).

NADIA KAMIL PROFILES MUSICIAN AND PERFORMER JUDITH OWEN

Honey Poo Poo and the Sad Songs of the Homesick

DEPENDING ON HOW YOU CAME ACROSS HER, JUDITH OWEN COULD STRIKE YOU as several different people. Her range of work throughout her career is like a hall of mirrors, each genre reflecting a slightly differently shaped person. Once you spend any time in the Judith Owen hall of mirrors, you soon realise that the singing-songwriting persona appears to be the most accurate image of her, and the clearest distillation of her talent.

Owen was born in London to Welsh parents, and says, 'I've been doing music since I was literally four years old.' Not surprising when you discover her father was a professional singer at the Royal Opera House, though she professes that she always wanted to be an actress so she 'never had to compete with him'. She followed that idea through and went to study at drama school, but soon realised the musician within her could not be ignored. In between acting classes, she would sit at a piano, as she had also done since she was four years old, and express herself through words and music. 'Music was the most pure thing I've ever done, the most direct thing into me,' she tells me. 'I thought for the longest time that no one would be interested in my very personal and interior songs.' It wasn't until she played some songs for a few friends that she cottoned on to the fact that her music was connecting with people and that it could, and should, be the focus of her career.

Owen's personal history is wrought in her work and this is especially evident in her latest release, *Ebb & Flow*, which she is currently touring. Following the death of her father she was spurred into creative action. She explains to me how the loss of a loved one makes you want to live, badly, and how she considered how she could possibly honour his life with her own. 'What would be a dream for me to do? Well, how about getting into a studio with the guys that I was listening to in the car as a kid with my mum and dad, singing along at the top of our lungs to James Taylor, Carole King and Joni? Wouldn't it be amazing if I made a record with them? That was my therapy.' So she did. Leland Sklar, Russ Kunkel and Waddy Watchel, a trio of hugely respected LA session musicians who have played for so many definitive

PHOTO: SUE FLOOD

artists, including those Owen had loved since those sing-along car journeys, agreed to record and tour the album with her.

The result is a record that exudes that classic 1970s West Coast personality which feels immediately familiar yet with a distinct Judith Owen touch. This album has been a long time in the making and is the culmination of Owen hitting her musical and emotional peak at the same time. Her career has seemingly careened about from playing the female foil for Richard Thompson, a live comedy cabaret show with Ruby Wax about mental illness and various projects with her husband Harry Shearer. And this all the while recording and releasing her own records.

It's clear that Owen enjoys collaboration and many types of performance and it's plain to see that Owen's calibre is reflected in the people who collaborate with her. 'I think you should do everything you're capable of as long as you're good at it,' she states confidently, informing me that she even created the artwork for the album. She certainly is good at it. Her comedic and playful side makes itself known in witty asides between tracks in her live shows and her social media accounts. Her Instagram account is full of knob jokes being blatantly enjoyed between her and bandmate Leland Sklar. One example is spun around a big penis-shaped yam, Yammy, their lucky mascot on the tour bus. 'I can't be that serious all the time, I think it's the flip side of being a dark person… the darkest people tend to be the people who need to laugh.'

Her dalliances with comedy are impressive, including an appearance as herself on *The Simpsons*, and the very fun-sounding *Judith Owen & Harry Shearer's Holiday Sing-Along*, which has attracted admirable guests including Jane Lynch and Christopher Guest. Her forays into comedy don't always match up to her prowess in music, however, as I found when watching the satirical web series she co-created with Shearer, *Honey Poo Poo*. This mini online series is a parody of the reality TV show, *Here Comes Honey Boo Boo*. It certainly showcases Owen's talent for performing big, silly characters, and is the result of being able to access everything in order to home-produce comic ideas. The downside here can be the lack of a critical eye, someone who might ask, 'What's the point? Is this more than a one-joke idea?' But the amount of fun the performers are having is so evident it's difficult to not be taken along with it.

It might be my fondness for the actual family that star in *Here Comes Honey Boo Boo* that makes me question what the target of this particular satire is. They're a family who obviously love each other and enjoy being in each other's company! That's adorable, isn't it? Who can resent that? I'm hoping that *Honey Poo Poo* is attempting to attack the increasing ludicrousness of reality TV shows rather than lampooning a sweet family who seem to have a great time mucking about with each other. However, I have to confess I've only seen one episode of *Here Comes Honey Boo Boo*, and that was on a plane, where for some reason I cry at pretty much everything I watch so my opinion of it is heavily filtered.

What we do get from *Honey Poo Poo*, however, is an unobstructed vision of the silly, playful side of Owen which stands in stark contrast to the earnest seriousness of her music. She says to me, 'I take my music very, very seriously,' and that is unambiguously obvious. But one facet of her music does hint at a more playful approach. Owen has a penchant for covering tracks and wholly making them her own. Often hugely well known songs, such as Deep Purple's 'Smoke On The Water' or Adele's 'Rolling in the Deep'. She says, 'Great songs are like great bones. You can hang whatever you want on them.' On *Ebb & Flow* she's recorded her own version of one of the most definitive summer songs that's ever been written, Mungo Jerry's 'In The Summertime'. This is a great example of how Owen luxuriates in fitting a classic song around her own shape, tailoring the recognisable fabric of the track into a new garment that suits her perfectly.

I wonder if this proclivity for making covers her own stems from the fact that Owen doesn't 'know where home is'. Her covers are an exercise comparable to moving to a new place and making it distinctively her own home. She describes herself as London Welsh, which is to say neither truly Welsh, nor truly a Londoner. She recalls that her happiest childhood memories are of their family trips to Wales, that she felt the biggest sense of belonging to a country she never lived in. I ask her if she knows the Welsh word *hiraeth* and she jumps on it, 'My dad used to say that to me, "Your songs are full of *hiraeth*." Owen feels she owes a lot to her motherland, she asserts that 'Wales makes great minor key music' which has influenced her songwriting sensibilities. She describes the Welsh as a 'glass-half-broken' type of people and that she 'inherited that sadness and yearning' which inspires a lot of great music. She's spoken about this with her sometime collaborator Richard Thompson, declaring that 'Great American folk music, sad, sad songs, come from people who are homesick.'

You sense Owen is destined to be forever homesick, being without a tangible, single place she can call home, other than music. I ask her if perhaps this is the reason she enjoys being on tour so much. 'If I could spend my life touring and performing, I'd be a very happy woman,' she replies. When I spoke to her she was in Nashville, excited to perform in a city with a strong musical history, and maybe even catch some bluegrass in her down time. Gathering to watch music being played live is as instinctive to Owen as she says it was to 'Primitive man.... That's how we're made.'

She describes touring as 'Like being on the best school trip you've ever been on, and you're the popular kid.' She thrives on live performance, she says she's a big believer in it. The shows on this spring's tour to promote *Ebb & Flow* are all free to attend. That decision is a canny one. Owen appreciates that at the moment many people might be struggling financially. In the world of music and live performance this can mean choosing between buying the music or attending a live show. Owen's smart decision to not charge for tickets is being rewarded with a lot of post-show CD and vinyl sales.

As a performer myself, I really respect that choice to open up the shows to anyone. To me, it's more important to have a room full of people excited to see and discover you than to make a few bucks from an audience who wonders if the show will be worth the ticket price. As Owen points out, 'People want to discover music, they want to find something they love and they want to support it.' This is an especially clever move for Owen as it is really in her physical performances that her songs come alive. She has said that she is the best accompanist for herself, and when you see her at the piano, it's hard to disagree. Owen is deliberate about this, she explains, 'The music I write is meant to be seen first and then heard on the record afterwards.'

Watching her sing her own songs is akin to witnessing her going through the emotions which created them. The effect is raw, the unpretentious lyrics about her own personal trials allow for a universal interpretation. Everyone in the audience makes their own connection with the tracks, then they buy the album after the show. It's hard for me to tell if the similarities between Judith Owen and myself are what made her music connect so directly or whether it is the skill of her song writing and performance that manages to speak so intimately to the listener.

The second song on *Ebb & Flow*, 'I Would Give Anything', explores Owen's reaction to her father's death, and nestled later in the album is 'You're Not Here Anymore', a song about her mother, who committed suicide when Owen was fifteen. My own mother died when I was young and this profound sense of loss in her songs sparks an almost visceral response in me. The darkness and light in Owen and her work strikes a balance that is to me both natural and familiar.

Rocked by her mother's loss, Owen has struggled with depression for much of her life. The disease appears to have played a big part in her life and her career. In 2010, Owen collaborated with Ruby Wax on a live stage show which directly dealt with their personal experiences of mental illness. Owen scored the show with songs embodying the feelings of Wax's comic narrative about her own breakdown. The show toured hospitals and institutions before a successful West End run.

Owen is an evangelist about the importance of openly discussing mental health issues. The second act of the show, a discussion with the audience, ended up acting as a sort of therapy for the people who attended. As Owen explains, 'It's an isolation that you cannot get through by yourself.' I ask her about the relationship, if any, between depression and creativity: she sees it as a dichotomy, like much of her career, and life itself. 'It's a double-edged sword. Life can be shit and wonderful at the same time... that's the meaning of *Ebb & Flow*. It's both things at once. Funny and sad. Wonderful and awful. Empty and full.'

Her depression has been the inspiration for much of her writing, and at the same time, music provided a life-line for her to deal with it. Writing songs could act as therapy. She tells me that 'Songs are my journals', a means to reach out and communicate her emotional struggles. Singing is one of those activities that releases chemicals that make you feel better, she says, like exercise. 'When choirs sing together their hearts start beating at the same time.' This biological response to the physical act of singing and of feeling better has solidified the connection between music and emotions for Owen. She acknowledges that sometimes getting to the point of being able to sing, or sit at a piano, can be a monumental struggle. The key for her is to be as open about it as possible. This is one of the reasons she has settled so well in America. When you tell an American you're in therapy, they don't raise an eyebrow. The British response often involves a classic stiff-upper lip and pretending you didn't hear whilst looking at your shoes. She still, however, loves Britain and frequently returns to savour our sense of humour and other cultural quirks America can't quite match.

Owen breathes this two-sided life. British and American. Silly and serious. Melancholy and joyful. The result is a pick and mix career: she is a bold, charismatic, silly, mischievous performer who sings deeply earnest, vulnerable and serious songs. 'I am the queen of the bittersweet song, everything is extremes to me. Gorgeous, awful, beautiful.' *Ebb & Flow* expresses a lot of that, but I distinctly get the feeling that to truly appreciate the work of this red-headed, wisecracking London Welsh, American transplant, it needs to be from the audience of a packed-out venue at one of her live shows. If only maybe to catch a glimpse of Yammy hanging out backstage.

Nadia Kamil *hails from Swansea and is a Welsh-Iraqi comedian, performer and writer. She has worked extensively in radio, especially with BBC Radio Wales, and performs solo stand-up across the UK and the London circuit. Last summer she performed her debut solo hour, 'Wide Open Beavers!', at the Stand III as part of the Edinburgh Fringe Festival and was hailed as being on the cusp of rising feminist comedy at the festival. She has also founded her own theatre company, Found Objects, has trained as a trapeze artist, and is currently training in aerial rope work.*

Fox Man

STORY BY **JAYNE JOSO**

ILLUSTRATION BY **JOERG RAINER NOENNIG**

TODAY I SAW THE MOST BEAUTIFUL HOUSE. TALL AND WIDE AND PAINTED WHITE. It stood alone, the others, all of brick. In fact, I almost did not see it, my eyes, so often of late, drawn to the ground. So now I pause and wonder whether it has been there very much longer than I realise, for I have surely walked that street before.

To each side of it the houses were perfect copies, one of another. Two storeys, in bricks of red, bay windows, twitchy curtains, a lone vase peeping out. Streets and streets, up and down, two storeys, bay windows, lonely vase.

I am between dwellings myself just now, on the lookout for a house. The place where I am staying is only temporary, and nice enough, but I shan't be there much longer. It's a shed.

By now I have passed the most beautiful house a great many times, and have begun to look a little closer. It seems there is never anyone about and so I have become quite bold. The corners of the house are smooth and rounded and the windows there are moulded, fitting these curves quite precisely. The sunlight splashes upon them and bounces back at me. But I cannot yet quite see inside (this will require some cunning and much closer inspection, and for that I had better take care, for were I to be seen, a wrong conclusion might be drawn.)

The curved windows appear to be entirely sealed, though I should just add that this is not conclusive, but merely, so far as I can tell without taking a ladder, and this I cannot do for fear of drawing attention to myself (it did cross my mind that I could take the part of a window cleaner, but I think I have wisely chosen against this since I can see how easily it could all go wrong.)

As for the back of the house, there are several points of access and yet it seems most likely that a house such as this must be heavily alarmed; but following some long days and evenings of close observation (though taking care to be casual and cautious in this endeavour), I can at least conclude with confidence that the house is currently uninhabited. And there is nothing to suggest that anyone is about to return soon; I would say quite the contrary, since I have noticed that the furniture is covered over with dust sheets. The owners, therefore, are away for some time.

The whole situation is by now quite frustrating, for lately I have started to feel a sense of responsibility for the fine dwelling. I have begun, under cover of the night sky, to tend the garden, since it is ever clear that there is no one here to do so. I have weeded all the garden over, turned the soil afresh, pruned the roses here (and there are many), and fed them at their base with finely chopped banana skins to give them back their life. And believe me now when I tell you, they will shortly bloom and bloom again! I have fixed the back fence, that intruders do not begin to find their way in; I have touched up the paintwork where required, and carried out other minor tasks, that the place does not fall into a state of disrepair. I have also cleaned the gutters.

Over the last few nights I have begun to worry about the property in my sleep, for a house as beautiful as this cries out to be lived in and loved, and really I would do that freely. I have, by now, overcome my fear of neighbours, possible questions, tittle-tattle or even accusations, for the windows simply cried out to be cleaned and this was labour for the daylight hours. Well, were you to see a child in the street with dirty cheeks and tears flowing from their eyes, would you deny them your handkerchief? No, and this is quite the same.

I don't know if anyone notices me, and I cannot say for certain whether anyone has spoken to me, for if they have it seems I do not hear.

It is all very well caring for a house such as this from the outside, and no one could be happier to do so than me, but really, I do need to get inside. I have tried to think what it might be like to own the place, how much it might cost to buy, and I have to question: would I have enough? And then there is the matter of the owners wanting to sell, which is quite another thing. It seems they ought to sell, or at the very least should consider as much since clearly no one lives here. But people rarely respond well to plain sense. *And why don't they live here?* Is the most beautiful house in their eyes somehow wanting, not enough? Not enough! What do people want if this is not enough? I am wrapped now, full body, about its curvilinear form. For even a house likes to be hugged. Am I strange? I beg you, do not answer.

Well, enough of that, there is still work to be done. At the top of this structure stands a glass house, so to say: a greenhouse. And I cannot begin to imagine what plants and vegetation lie suffering there in the heat. I will find a way up.

It is with a tragic heart, that I tell now of the death of a whole summer's produce lying in the hot house. What were they thinking, to abandon this place so? I had no choice but simply to remove the overripe and rotting matter, and to begin the labour of cleaning out the greenhouse in quite a thorough manner. I will replace all this dead material with lovely fresh soil and best it is planted anew. It is a deal of work and in such great heat; the ladder somewhat precarious. There is access from the inside certainly, but I do not have a key. No matter, I make the best of things. And over the weeks I can now quite boldly claim that a truly substantial amount of work has been done here. A labour of love on my part. Making my beautiful house precisely so.

I own a large round tin, so large it can hold quite a fortune. And when the owners return I am hoping that it might just be enough to secure the place, a sizeable deposit at the very least. It seems that the owners of such a wonderful dwelling must surely be the most reasonable kind, for to have such taste is certainly a measure of character.

Time moves on, and the seasons quickly change. Before long I will have fallen leaves to deal with and all the labours of late autumn will be upon me. I must consider how best to protect the plants and home from the colder months to come. It is bizarre to me, to leave a place such as this so very alone, but it has given me a great deal of comfort and I have been supremely happy to have made its acquaintance. And when finally I take up residence here it is certain to be a whole new adventure, a sense of coming home.

They're back. I was not entirely sure of this when I came by this morning (I had intended to do some work here when I noticed a vehicle in the driveway, perhaps officials checking on the place), but now I am quite certain that it is the owners returned. They are a couple, a man and a wife. They have two dogs, a dashing Dalmatian and the sweetest Jack Russell I have ever seen. What a thing! To own the most beautiful house and two of the most handsome dogs that ever lived.

I have returned to the shed, wasting not a single moment, and have hastily pulled on my smartest jacket and dusted off my tin of treasure, I can only hope it will be enough to make a good impression and assure them of my serious intention. There are holes in the soles of my shoes, but never mind, when I am upright these cannot be seen.

It is with a particular joy that I waltz back up to the house just now, sure in the knowledge that I will no longer need to fret about how I will manage another winter in the shed, and confident of my offer.

My heart is pounding, fast and vital. I have knocked at the door and wait here smiling warmly, the owner grows large behind the glass. The door draws in, and as it does so I feel the sensation of a fanfare, as though a great new chapter is being ushered in. A line of trumpets sounds.

With outstretched arms I offer the man the tin and explain, perhaps a little too quickly and excitedly, my intentions. He looks perplexed and I encourage him to open the tin. Open the tin!

He does so, and I wait patiently for his reaction.

'Buttons,' he says, 'just buttons.'

I find I do not speak, and struggle to understand his response, or rather his lack of response, but perhaps he too is searching for words (this happens to me quite often, especially during episodes of over-excitement).

He has replaced the lid and passed the tin back to me. His look is stern as he marks where I stand, communicating in his stare that I would not be welcome were I to move closer. I hold the tin in my arms as though it were a child sleeping. The Dalmatian regards me from deep inside the house. I cannot see the Jack Russell but hear a scratching that suggests him. And then a whimper.

'Just buttons,' the man says again. 'You cannot buy a house with buttons.'

I hold on tight to the tin. He shuts the door and is gone. And there is no sound, he does not call to his wife, there are no footsteps heard, no barks or whimpers from the dogs deep within. Not a thing. Nothing at all. He is quite simply gone.

Jayne Joso *grew up in north Wales and has since lived and worked in Japan, China and Kenya. Primarily a novelist and playwright, she is author of* Soothing Music for Stray Cats *and* Perfect Architect, *both published by Alcemi. She was awarded the Coracle, Ireland, International Writer's Residency in 2012; and in 2013 her poem, 'Desire', was purchased by MoMa, New York, as part of the Abe's Penny Archive. Her next novel, set in Tokyo, received the Great Britain Sasakawa Foundation Award. jaynejoso.uk. @JayneJoso*

STORY BY **JOAO MORAIS**

Plunder

EIGHT LABOURER'S COTTAGES. KNUCKLED AND WHITEWASHED AND DAMP. SUNDAY trew for the job, and his only pair with pockets at that. The town is at Church and Chapel. Quick are Grayson's feet up the garden path, but quiet he creeps along. Not a siw or a miw past the gate and the hedge and the kale.

He breathes in. The sweet herb scent of burning wet wood. The birth of the stillborn morning. This is what he's thinking. Not of Grace. Not of what happens if he gets caught. Another conviction and the fine will be crippling.

The back door to the third is not barred. It opens into a bedroom. Not even a filled chamber pot under the bed. A door to the right. The long slate in the pantry. A hunk of cheese goes in his inside pocket.

Into the parlour. He looks around. Embers on the grate. A bowlen of dried flowers. Her Majesty's dour jowls in a frame. The diamond-stencilled paper peeling off the wall. He finds the port on the dresser shelf and takes the last swig. There's no time. Pewter cups on the mantelpiece. Ornaments either side, a pair of twisted purple roses. The kind of thing Grace loves. He puts them in his pockets. It's a Sunday. No chance of selling to someone who doesn't care. It's not enough but they'll have to do.

Outside and he swaggers back down the old Penparcau road, thinking of where to raid next. Wondering how long Grace will remain stable. He's looking beyond at the smooth tumble of hills and that's why he almost misses the Stranger. He's walking towards him. The only two men not indoors praying.

Grayson feels uneasy when they get closer. The Stranger looks like he knows something. Eyes sharper than Shropshire cider. The uncircumcised lips of a fish. Flame-bright hair but not like anything from Rosslare Harbour. You could tell he was hot for the clecs. They nod heads and move on. When Grayson gets to the bridge he looks back. The Stranger is looking back too.

Ling-di-long he walks through town. Trying to forget the Stranger, roughly heading back home. Or summoning up the courage at least. The sun blasts the heat onto his face. Roasting his skin to a darker shade of white. When he gets to the High Street the breeze brings a poster. He reads it out loud to himself and folds it up to fit in his pocket. At least he has the next job.

Two minutes later and he pauses before thumbing the catch on his own front door, and breathes in. His wife is on the settle, staring at the fire. She turns her head. He stares at the muddy clasp of hair that clings to her scalp.

– What did you get?, she says.

He puts the cups on the table, and they hear Grace coughing. Mary doesn't need to know about the ornaments.

– Can't do anything with that, she says. – It's a Sunday. All we can do is add them to the pile.

– It's all we have till later, he says, and pulls the cheese from his inside pocket.

She smiles at the welcome sight of the cheese. The scalded teeth of a habitual smoker. She gets up and strides forward. Each stomp ends with a wheeze.

She takes it and breaks off half and halves it again. She gives him the smallest piece, takes a small piece to her own mouth. The larger chunk put on the table.

– Save the rest for when Grace gets better, she says.

He doesn't want to think about Grace.

– I need the Rector's wine, he says. – Must be some left. We didn't drink every bottle.

She looks up at him. Her C-shaped back pulled into shape by her pendulum breasts.

– We should sell the last one. Get some medicine, she says.

– It's a Sunday. Need hard cash. And there's only one place that will have cash on a Sunday.

Her cheeks and nose shine back. He can almost see his face.

– I shall not visit Bow Street again, she says. – A pox on that cursed village and all who enter it.

– No need for that, he says. – The bank doesn't open till tomorrow. Took cash last night then it best be looked after proper. Give me the bottle and I'll show you something.

They stare at each other, but she breaks first.

– You can have one swig, she says. – One swig and then no more. Please have but one swig.

She might nag but he still admires his wife. As wordy and brave as any Bristol preacher. There's still something between them, perhaps; a sweat-pore of attraction left.

Mary goes up the stairs. He can hear her murmur to Grace through the coughing. The crumpled sound of limbs mean she's getting down on her knees. The bottle under the bed. Using the ill child who must not be disturbed.

She comes down and puts the wine on the table. You can tell she's been at it from the sloshing. He takes it in his hand and uncorks it. Not even half full. A long smooth swig.

– Ych a fuckin fi, he says. – This is awful.

Arthur Grayson, Romford, Sussex. Theatricalist, was fined 2 / and costs at Aberystwyth on the 16th September 1899 for having stolen paste ornaments from St Philips hall, Aberystwyth.

PHOTO: DIGIDO PROJECT, THE NATIONAL LIBRARY OF WALES

– Never make a local, you won't, she says, and takes the pewter cups for hiding. – Cursing like that. Surprised you're not well known to the law already.

He takes the poster from his pocket. She reads it as he takes another swig.

Professor George Black, proprietor of Black's Wax Works.
A New Novelty For The Pleasure of the townsfolk of ABERISTWITH;
At St Phillip's Hall
FOR ONE NIGHT ONLY
An Intensely Pleasing Programme Deserving Of The Heartiest Praise
With Musical Accompaniment

– This is no plan, she says. – There won't be anything there. It'll be with the Professor or in the hotel safe. You can't break into a hotel.

– There will be something, he says. – No-one cleans up after any Saturday event until Church the next morning.

She takes the wine off him and swigs. The last mouthful. – You have to go now, Grace needs her medicine. You know what the Doctor said. And they only talk outside after the service for so long.

It's a joke. People think you're an expert breaker if you just find the right door to bang in the right place. He goes round the back of the hall and tries the double doors. Locked from the inside. But the cellar grate is loose and he's in. Up the stairs in the black, and hip-bashing through two rooms.

He gets in the main hall, silhouetted with the Professor's figures. You can barely see with the blinds down.

He looks around before deciding what to take. Professor Black is not Madame Tussaud. He spies a Maid Marian that used to be a Robin Hood. You can tell by the square of her jaw. Next is a warning sign in front of a velvet curtain. Behind on a horse sits Lady Godiva. For some unknown reason, a Savage from the Congo is guarding. Jack the Ripper stands near, bent over and cloaked and Jewish. Professor Black's sly sense of humour. Everyone knows it was the Duke of Clarence.

Poor Grace. The poor dwt. Only saleable things for a Monday. No coin for a Sunday. No credit good will available from the Doctor after the disgrace of last time. And Mary too stupid or too proud to beg for credit from the neighbours. She'll have to visit the horrors of Bow Street at this rate.

He takes the timepiece from Gladstone's pocket. The hipflask from Livingstone's belt. Swaps shoes with Beethoven. All the little things that Professor Black won't notice. And that's when he sees him. The mad Corsican. Napoleon sits at the war table in his stupid bicorn hat. A map of Europe in front of him. Wooden pawns along the English Channel. Eight bottles of wine to the sides.

He hurries over. Dust on the neck of each. All empty save two. The chipped battered cork of a hundred seaside towns. He pushes down hard and steady with his middle finger. A minute of effort and it is swimming in the brine.

He swigs until the drink rolls down his neck. Another and he is gasping and the bottle is empty.

He thinks about pressing the other, but the wine hits the pit of his stomach and his head goes giddy and he feels like voiding. This hoard of junk won't be enough. There must be a coin or two on the floor. Anything to make Grace better.

He's wandering around by the big arched entrance doors. He can't believe it. In the corner on a low table, a till underneath a calico shroud. He tries picking it up but it's too heavy. Professor Black the lazy bastard.

He gets out a file and stabs the keyhole. Nothing doing. He goes back to Napoleon and takes a bottle. Butts the file and the lock snaps. Turns easy and he's in. Puts the bottle back and checks the register.

Heartstop. A full till. He weeds a hand through the receding part of his scalp. He starts to fill his pockets but fills them too quickly. Still half a tray left.

He goes back to Napoleon. Takes his stupid hat. Grayson empties his pockets into it. Empties the till and shuts it. Knots the calico shroud round the tinny sound of the coins in the bicorn.

He traces his steps, harder now that the wine has hit his head. Puts the grating back. Stuffs the hat down the back of his Sunday trew. Turns two corners heading the half a mile back towards home when he sees the Stranger from earlier. The top of the Stranger's head like a newly struck match.

He's forty yards away. – There's your man, he says, and Grayson realises that he's not alone this time. A stiff broad constable behind him. The thick thoroughbred neck of the law.

Grayson is drunk and panics. Full of the Stranger's port and the Rector's awful pish and Napoleon's war room wine. He turns and makes for a corner. Turns another and almost brings up the last bottle. Looks behind and they've made ten yards. The constable has his truncheon out.

There's only one thing for it. He has to think of Grace. The only advantage. He gets near his own street and they're both lagging. At least he has fifteen years on them. He turns left. A dash down the lane at the back. He counts the houses by name. Past the Reagans, the two house Evans. Mrs Pritchard and her stovepipe hat. Two more and he's at his own, and Napoleon's bicorn flies over the wall. Mary will hear and hide it in the pile with the cups. She must hear.

He turns right and goes to turn back on himself down his own street, but comes round the corner into the Stranger's fist. Socked on the cheek and hitting the wall and the world is turning sideways.

He's being grabbed and held down. He can feel the Stranger's knee in his back. Can't even rub his own jaw, just about able to grunt and struggle. The Stranger is not a big man. Elbows that you could circle with a thumb and finger. But Grayson can't move at all.

The constable approaches. Built for bashing, not for running. Leans against the wall while he asks Grayson what the hell he's playing at.

– Look, he's drunk, the Stranger says. – I told you, he drunk the last of my port. Took my pewter cups.

– What have you got to say for yourself? the constable says.

– Useless pieces of junk, Grayson answers. – Weren't worth taking. True as the Bible, I am.

While the Stranger holds Grayson down the constable empties his pockets. They find the watch and Grayson insists it's a family heirloom. They find the hip flask and the Constable mutters that no wonder they can smell the booze on his breath. And then they find the ornaments. Two purple roses, glazed and baked. The ones he was saving for Grace.

It's enough to press charges, but it could be worse.

The constable and the Stranger take an arm each behind Grayson's back towards the station. Gladstone won't miss his watch. Livingstone's hip flask was empty anyhow. All they can do him on is a few old paste ornaments. Overnight in a cell and the Magistrates in the morning, and he's got the fine covered now. And enough for Grace's medicine too. Even enough for Mary to start afresh when Professor Black finds out.

This story was inspired by the photograph, pictured on p27, from the National Library of Wales digital archive, Cardiganshire Constabulary Register of Criminals, 1897–1933, llgc.org.uk/index.php?id=criminals.

João Morais *is studying for a PhD in Creative Writing at Cardiff University. A nominee for the 2009 Rhys Davies Short Story Competition, he won the Terry Hetherington Award in 2013. His work appears in* Nu2: Memorable Firsts, *amongst other publications.*

A Minor Accident on the Way to Buy Toothpaste

In the UK, two to three people become paralysed as a result of a spinal cord injury, every single day.

THE TEENAGE YEARS WERE OVER, BOTH SONS WERE SAFELY ENSCONCED AT St Andrew's University and they were happy and healthy. I had untied my apron strings and relaxed my guard. Then, on a summer's day in 2004, my youngest son was involved in a minor accident on a country road on the way to buy toothpaste. It was no more than a shunt really: the other three people were unhurt, but sitting in the back and not wearing a seat belt, Jack's head hit the roof of the car, which broke his neck, paralysing him from the chest down.

What came next has been movingly documented in Melanie Reed's 'Spinal Column' in *The Times*. But what happens when the doctors and nurses and physiotherapists and social workers and psychiatrists have done all they can? What happens when the disabled person comes home?

This 'disabled person' was our twenty-two-year-old son. He had a future, though not the one we had all expected, and many adaptations had to be made, both practical and emotional. It was dealing with the necessary changes to the house that first helped us to cope with the emotional turmoil and our growing apprehension as the day for Jack's return from hospital grew near.

Luckily we already lived in a bungalow, so the conversion for a wheelchair user was not as complicated as for some. We needed permanent ramps at the front and back of the house for wheelchair access. Door handles needed to be lowered and altered so that with limited hand function he could let himself in or out of the house. The guest bathroom was converted into a wet-room and the wall between it and his bedroom knocked through.

The wheelchair icon, the one printed over the door of public toilets and in designated parking places, is what most people 'see' when they think of disability, so we weren't prepared for all the unseen paraphernalia or 'aids'. When Jack came home for good after nine months in hospital, he wheeled himself up the decking ramp to the front door. His bedroom and newly converted wet-room were in place. So was an electrically operated bed with a special mattress, a portable hoist, a toileting wheelchair, a standing frame, a sliding board, a supply of incontinence sheets, boxes of leg bags (day and night), catheters, enemas and assorted drugs for spasms and nerve pain.

At first we needed all of this, and more. Our day would start in the middle of the night when his father or I would wake him to help him turn in the bed. A district nurse would have visited the previous evening to administer 'bowel care', so in the morning I would clean him and change the bedding. His night bag would be disconnected, unfastened from the bed and emptied and then a day bag attached to his penis with a convine and the bag strapped to his leg. It took several weeks of trial and error to find a make of convine which didn't slip off. Using his remote control he could raise his mattress to sit himself up, then a young girl from a care agency would arrive to dress him and help him into the wheelchair with the aid of the hoist.

The first months were a strange and intimate time. Just before the accident I had been talking to Jack and one of his friends. He had been wearing a wetsuit top and his torso had been so muscular and strong that I laughingly patted it and said, 'I made that.' Now he would let me wash, turn and dress him as he lay there in his youth, maleness and beauty. He didn't look broken or damaged; this was what was so heart-breaking. Nor was there a sense of paralysis as his legs still moved involuntarily. His body looked as if it were ready for life and love and fatherhood and action and running.

There are seven vertebrae in the neck numbered from C1, the highest, to C7. When Jack's head hit the roof of the car on that sunny morning, he injured his neck at the C5/C6 level. It would have been easy to look for precise details of what activities were still possible after similar injuries. For example, *Functional Outcomes per Level of Spinal Cord Injury* would have told me that patients like Jack 'can dress their upper body and assist with lower body dressing'. It was just as well that I didn't do this research, as every patient is different, if only in small ways.

At an early stage in his 'recovery', Jack told us that we didn't have to turn him in the night any more; he would set his alarm clock and manage it on his own. In time he also devised a way of levering himself into a sitting position without needing to use the bed's controls. This seemed to involve a furious expenditure of energy, but he persevered. The next piece of high-tech equipment to become redundant was the hoist, which was replaced with a sliding board. A decidedly low-tech item, this is a flat, boomerang-shaped piece of highly polished wood. One end is pushed under the patient's bottom as he sits on the bed and the other end is placed on the seat of the wheelchair. Then, using the remaining triceps in his arms, Jack could slide across. This method of transfer had been practised in the months of physiotherapy and was to become the way he moved from chair to car or made any other transfer.

I had often wondered how it was that we could walk on the moon, land a probe on Mars and photograph the origins of the universe and yet not find better solutions for Jack's incontinence. Intermittent catheterization is a solution but needs a fine degree of hand and finger function, which Jack does not possess. However, once again he persevered and the boxes of leg bags were put away to be kept for emergencies. It took much longer to discover a routine which settled his bowel function, but eventually he discovered that a visit from the district nurse every other morning and the use of the toileting chair worked well.

Jack left the Spinal Unit in May 2005 and set himself the target of finishing his degree at St Andrews, commencing in October of the following year. He would need to learn to drive, and after one false start, we found an instructor who had a car with the suitable adaptations. Acceleration and breaking are performed with a special lever, using the left wrist, and the right hand wears a glove with a spike attached, which fits into a hole in the steering wheel. Lights and windscreen wipers are automatic and indicators are triggered by a series of clicks on a rocker-switch. To our delight, he passed on his second attempt, but there were still months of practice to enable him to slide from his chair into the driver's seat, bring the sliding board into the car, dismantle his chair, lift the pieces across into the passenger seat and then reverse the process once he arrived at his destination.

Jack completed the autumn term at St Andrews, but despite the best efforts of the university to provide him with the help he needed, he decided that he had had enough. He had gone armed with the latest technology: a laptop, recorders for lectures, a voice recognition device and his own specially adapted car. With hindsight, what he'd needed was a full-time 'buddy' or carer, so that he didn't exhaust himself getting in and out of the car; someone who could get to the library in time for him to access the books he needed for the next week's tutorial, indeed, someone who could turn the pages of the heavy books he was referencing. Jack's marks that term started to reduce the grade-point average he had built up with such pride and care over the previous three years: he lost interest in history, the subject that had fascinated him since he was a small child – and that was that. It was then that his father and I finally acknowledged that Jack would never resume, even in a limited way, the life he had before.

If we were tempted to grieve for one more loss, Jack quickly undeceived us. I have often thought about how we would have coped if Jack had become permanently depressed after his accident or if he had railed against his fate and wanted to die. You read of such cases. Alternatively, there are astonishing accounts of paraplegics and even tetraplegics who become athletes, climb mountains, ski down them, or sail the Atlantic. Jack did none of these things. Once again, he seemed to shrug his shoulders, accept that he didn't actually need a degree anymore, and just got on with his life, back with his parents.

He has now reached a sort of plateau as far as his physical 'improvement' is concerned. The days when I had to care for his intimate bodily needs are over. He no longer falls from his chair very often or needs help to get in and out of bed. At some time in the future, there will be a decline, and the hoist and even the electric bed will be needed again, but who ever knows what the future will bring?

Nothing is straightforward, and we quickly learned about the less well-known complications of a high spinal injury. The most serious of these is autonomic dysreflexia, a life-threatening emergency characterized by a sudden increase in blood pressure. It can be caused by a blocked bowel or bladder, or even an ingrowing toenail; something which would normally cause discomfort below the level of the injured spinal cord. This stimulates nerve impulses to travel up the spinal cord, until the lesion at the point of injury blocks them. The result is a dangerous rise in blood pressure and other, very unpleasant symptoms.

Then there is the possibility of bedsores. Last year, Jack had to spend a month lying on his stomach, to cure a sore caused originally by an ingrowing hair. Kidney and bladder stones are a common side effect of being confined to a wheel chair. Jack can no longer cough or sneeze very well; but he can laugh. Another bizarre result of an injury like Jack's is the inability to regulate his body temperature. He must never again sit in the hot sun for longer than a few minutes.

Yet as I write this apparently bleak account, I can hear Jack's voice from his room. He's laughing and talking on his computer as he plays *World of Warcraft*. This summer he spent a weekend in Italy, meeting all his friends from the game.

Jack has a life, and he seems content. He is blessed with many local friends who often visit him. It's almost like an extended adolescence: I can come home to find a gang of lads in his room – these 'lads' now approaching thirty years of age – watching a film, gossiping and drinking beer. He will drive to the cinema or go out for a meal and he leads a life that is not dependent on his parents' company. He is dependent on us, of course, and we are lucky to have still his witty, amusing and cheerful company. Sometimes, I think about Anna, the girl he was in love with at the time of the accident, and what his life might have been now, if only.... I also remember the day when he was called out as crew on the local lifeboat to rescue a family cut off by the tide. But I watch, less frequently, the video of him taken by a friend, a week before the day everything changed, where he is doing cartwheel after cartwheel, and laughing into the camera.

Names and other details have been changed to protect the privacy of 'Jack'.

Ellie Rees *is studying for a PhD in Creative Writing at Swansea University. Before that she was Head of Languages at Atlantic College in the Vale of Glamorgan, and lived and worked there for twenty-seven years.*

STORY BY **CANDY NEUBERT**

Monthly Payments

SIX MONTHS BEFORE, DIANE CAME IN AND PUT THE SHOPPING ON THE TABLE, exactly like that. He said, 'The hospital rang; he's not well.' Straight away she knew who it was, even though they never mentioned him, ever.

She put the shopping on the table now. It was eerily the same, as if they were reconstructing a scene for the police. Her thin shoulders in the same red coat, the bags dropped to the table, Morrisons and Tesco and the green canvas one, A Bag For Life.

Brian opened the fridge and put the cold stuff away. He made tea, covering the pot with the blue tea cosy with sprigged flowers, a link with his mother. Finally he sat on the back doorstep, looking down the garden, while Diane took off her coat and her town shoes, and rinsed the cups.

She might come and join him; he'd like it if she did. She could bring the tea and sit next to him on the step, resting her knee against his, sharing his tobacco and a lighted match.

He heard the tea, poured out. The newspaper was unfolded, there was a pause; she handed his cup over his shoulder.

'Thanks', he said.

'Mm', she replied. But she didn't join him. After a moment he heard her leave the kitchen, and presently a chair scraped the floor of the front room. She'd be sitting down in there, doing the charity shop books.

There were a lot of books this time; Brian collected them from the recycling centres once a month. Perhaps this time she'd find one or two for herself. She took the first one from the nearest pile and checked the cover, front and back. Then she set it down and gazed out of the window.

It was the boy's birthday today; of course she had remembered. Even though the boy was now dead, it was still his birthday and Brian was feeling it. He'd be thinking about it, sitting on the step with his tea. She could have sat there with him, saying nothing; even the cat would do as much, if either of them was troubled.

The garden was coming back to life, the daffodils up, the ends of the lilac fat with green. It had been the garden she couldn't leave when they might have made a clean break and moved away. New owners would strip the house and start again. They might dig the garden over and turn it all to lawn, or add decking with an outdoor heater like the Marlows at number 26. In the end she and Brian had stayed; it was her decision, as everything was.

She thought of their bedroom, how it might be changed. The wall into the spare room could be knocked through, or the spare turned into a bathroom; people liked a bathroom to be upstairs. It would happen one day after they went into a nursing home, or died, or whatever lay ahead.

The first book in front of her was a cookery one, brand new. There was often a clearing out at this time of year, cookery, gardening, sport. She kept the gardening ones until the next batch; it didn't matter. Grubby covers she wiped clean, pencil marks she rubbed out, those with missing pages went into the paper bin. Brian would take them to the RSPCA shop when she had finished.

'Still thinking of risotto?'

'There weren't any mushrooms. Not fresh ones. I got a pepper. There's quiche, if you'd rather.'

'I'll do risotto. Shall I?'

'If you want. I don't mind doing it.'

'I don't mind either.'

A novel next, *Death in Summer*, quite good condition. She put it out of sight; there was no need to hurt him and she'd never wanted to do so. It had been summer last year when the boy died. Summer, too, eleven years before, when she'd emptied Brian's trouser pockets ready for the wash, his college trousers always washed at the weekend and the pockets usually turned out by himself, but not this once.

They discussed that, why he hadn't emptied his pockets, if subconsciously he needed to be found out. They brought the subject painfully to the surface like the shards of a wreckage, upstairs in the middle of the night while Brian's cigarette burned in the dark and she curled on her side with her back to him. Layers of it were still coming up, like mucus.

Eleven years ago, she ran her hand through his pocket and drew out a folded paper. When she had read it, she sat down on the bed and listened. The radio was on downstairs, there was birdsong in the garden. After a while she took the trousers with the rest of the wash and filled the machine. She turned the radio off, rolled a cigarette and read the letter again. Later, when Brian came home, she pushed it across the table towards him.

A simple story, old as the hills. She used the phrase in her mind, as old as the hills: middle-aged ex-hippy takes up teaching and has affair with student. News of a baby was also a cliché, but that was the core of it, the sound she had heard behind the birdsong and the radio, her own life rending open.

Brian gathered the ingredients. Pepper, garlic, onions, his own tomatoes from the crop grown against the back wall last year, their pulp frozen. He needed to be useful until he went back to his job; he was on compassionate leave, reasons unspecified. It had been written up in the *Shropshire Star* at the time, an unusual death.

He took the chopping board from the drainer and cut the onions. Olive oil from the cupboard, Napolina medium flavour. Rice, seasoning, salt, flaked almonds, a little extra, just a few, a gift. As he scraped onion into the oil, the phone rang.

'Hello?' he said. 'Ah yes. I'll just see.'

Diane appeared in the doorway, the habitual crease between her eyebrows very noticeable, like a knot.

'No,' she mouthed silently, her hands making a flat, downward movement. 'No, no.'

'Er, sorry,' he said into the phone. 'I thought she was here, but she must've popped out. Shall I ask her to call you? Oh, okay. Yes, I will. Okay. Bye. Bye, then.' He replaced the receiver. 'Mary. About the concert. She's bringing a programme.'

'What, *now*?'

'Yes, she's on her way to collect something or other. Wants to know, are you going to the fireworks again this year?'

'No, I'm not.'

'Oh God, the onions.'

The books were finished, piled on the right of the table now instead of the left. She put *Death in Summer* on the top shelf where Brian would never see it. She might read it when he went back to work, if he ever did.

She began to pack each pile into a cardboard box. Mary was coming. She folded the flaps of cardboard over and then remained where she stood. The mantel clock was suddenly apparent, as if it only ticked now and then, and not all the time.

Mary was coming. That was a bad thing. Not that there was anything wrong with Mary, nothing at all; she was perfectly nice. Why was she coming, though? It was like being caught, caged, knowing somebody was coming; it was a bird in her chest, beating up her throat. Diane touched her throat, where she felt it.

'Is she walking or coming by car?'

'Who?'

'Mary. You said she's coming. I'm going out. I don't know which way she's coming. Walking or car?'

'She didn't say. I presumed walking, but maybe she'll drive; I don't know. How do I know? Have we any of those pine nuts left?'

'I've got to go.' Diane picked up her coat. 'If she turns up, I'm out.'

She was like that, now. In the early days she'd never minded people, though she didn't want children and he said neither did he, without giving it any thought. He never thought about it all the years in the building trade, or when he gave that up because of his asthma, or while he retrained as a teacher and began to teach woodwork in schools during the day and evening classes for adults, one of whom was called Rachel. He never thought about wanting children even when he allowed himself to have Rachel; he was forty-two at the time, these things happen.

When she, Diane, had pushed the letter across the table – this same table he now wiped with a cloth – while he stared at it blankly she jumped up and left the house. She was gone for hours. Long after dark she returned to find him packing his clothes. I thought you'd want me to go, he said. She replied, 'There's no need for that.'

Gentle Diane, shy Diane, the girl with a soft voice and blonde hair and long Indian skirts. The blonde hair had grown fluffy and so pale it was impossible to say at what point it was turning white. They were both in their fifties now.

She walked rapidly through the town towards the canal. She must not see Mary. If she saw her she would kill her, she felt the need of it, the need to get rid of the threat by any means. Anyone who came to the house and pinned her into it, was a threat. Mary wasn't important, she was nobody. It made no difference – family, friends, anyone; if they crossed a certain line it was too late forever, she would extinguish them, freeze them off the face of the earth, she couldn't help it.

No need for that, she'd said. Did he want to leave? Well, then. She was perfectly clear and composed, waiting beside him as he dialled Rachel's number, her eyes wide open, shining with concentration. Perfectly composed when Rachel knocked on their door later that evening. She watched Rachel's dismay with curiosity and distaste, but without malice. She forbade Brian to leave the room.

Rachel was entitled to have the child, she said, and Brian must support it. Rachel would notify them of the birth; monthly payments would begin forthwith by direct debit until the child was eighteen. That was the law. Brian would in no way act as father and he would not see Rachel again.

He had a blurred memory of the whole thing. He'd covered his face with his hands, appalled by the words *notify* and *forthwith*, while Diane saw Rachel to the door.

Years later he was conscious that he was happier, knowing that he had a son.

He continued to teach, including the evening classes, needing the money. He and Diane remained as before; for a while he thought they were closer, often having long conversations in the dark. They never mentioned the boy, how old he must be, or what he might be like. He and his mother had moved to Ketley, so there was no likelihood of meeting.

She hurried now past Brooklyn's Cleaners and Paws Whole Petfoods. Everyone wanted a bit of her, wanted her to open her mouth and talk rubbish and to listen to their rubbish in return. And all the while Brian had bypassed her body and swum into eternity through some other, random woman.

But six months ago he said, 'He's not well,' and they went all the way to the hospital. The woman Rachel was unrecognizable, her blunt face messy with grief. Brian, his teeth chattering with a kind of tremor, ran his hands across the dead child, over and over. Cardiomyopathy, they said. No way of telling. One minute playing football, next minute gone.

She reached the canal out of breath, just as a pair of ducks disappeared under the bridge. That person Mary would have been and gone by now; it was safe to go back. Brian could fend them all off now. He'd have the bowls ready on the table, perhaps a candle, and a lid on the risotto, keeping it warm.

---

*Having published two novels with Seren (*Foreign Bodies *and* Big Low Tide*),* ***Candy Neubert*** *has come back to short stories and poetry. She was Poet in Residence for the National Trust in 2013, judge of the Guernsey International Poetry Award in 2014, and remains a regular contributor to* The Spectator.

PHILIP GROSS

The River Next Door

Taff valley, Quakers Yard

1. The garden comes down to the river...

with drowned corn-dolls
of flood-wrack in the wire,
    our fiction of a border,
the last post up-torn,
    up-tangled, rammed back
at an angle in the grey silt
    with baroque scrunched lager cans,
one flip-flop, and a corrugated
    rust-fret fine as peeled bark,

while what's left of the fence
    drift-nets the stream
snagging quick shreds of blue
    cement bags slim as fish.
(There *are* fish, too, like sinewy
    dreams, head on and fighting
upstream home to Merthyr.)

2. The Water Table

All summer it lazed
                on its stone-bed – half
the autumn too. Rain barely stirs it. Only

up, under the hills,
                in the dark long (centuries-
long) hall weight shifts, the water table

being laid: the not-
                yet-woken guests'
cups fill, are filled, are running over. Then

the day. A meadhall
                clamour. Rain sheets
off the fields, the glistening flanks. It spills

into present-time, smells
                sour, knows no bounds,
remembers too much and will not be stilled.

3. The house wants to go back...

to the river. It breathes
water up through its bones

in shadows, small bouquets
of salts, crisp-dusty on the plaster.

Windows grow weepy. Mortar,
wearied, with its lime leached out

by rising damp and time
reverts to stream-bed gravel

that trickles away, leaving nubs
of raw river-stone, blunt

from the hard knocks
of the flood beach, only roughly settled:

an accommodation
to each other and to gravity

we call a house.
Where its corset of render has buckled,

it's been patched and cracks again.
Tap here or here, or here, a hollowness

responds – blown resonating spaces
like a Greek mask, an appalled

or gurning jar-head, face
to the amphitheatre's empty rows,

much as we address the far slope,
Cefn Glas with that velvety green

of a written-out slag heap –
the mute knowledge how one nearby

hillside changed one day
losing its grip, dissolving inwardly

(a long-buried spring and one too many
days of rain) as it let itself go

like a black sigh, coal-slurry and grit-sludge,
only wanting to be river

but there was a village in the way.

4. A coal pebble

: greyish, with a slight glint at one angle, not quite
stone, but oval and wafery, light to the touch.
(Skimmed low, it could walk on the water
almost, right up to that panicky
teeter at the end.)

It comes clean as any other from the river, as if
innocent – bland, black and innocent – of what it did.
What it left. (Not just under the hills
here but under the valley,
the Deep Navigation

past saving, sealed, filling with emptiness, drip
by rising drip like a glass harp (séance music,
its inhuman purity of tone). A cave-diver
might yet stoop and crawl
through the long sump

dragging his budget of air behind him, half
astronaut, half miner of that worked-out near-
unreachable inner space, peering
into the night of the male
soul, a lamp in his hat.)

5. What's to do with it

: that old muscle and wit
with which the Taff rises? Mad
bad pranks, extreme japes, anything

(like the kids who torch the bracken
leaving slim birch saplings ashen-
white and shrivelled) just to make a mark....

I found three bicycles, a rust-contraption
wrangling in the shallows, twisted into one another
in a circus strongman's knot.

I lost count of the draggled buggies
that beached awhile, then bumped by
like a skeleton pram-push, jolt by nudge

for years, quixotic, off
to blight the views of Cardiff Bay.
And the bikes? I waded in, all good intentions,

tugged and slipped and swore. Gave up
on recycling. Looked around, then
kicked them back

to what the river wanted. Waved them on their way.

6. It's nothing personal...

the damp of this land, the way it rises. Or
not *rises – finds its level*. The hills
are a column of water

that each autumn fills to the skyline. Each
slope of the valley is a green-
brown standing wave

like you see in a tide-rip, constant pressure,
isobars in tons per square inch,
the soil's weather.

What made you think you could live here
dryshod? (Or so says the soul-
surveyor. My full

report will follow in due course. And the bill.)

7. A River Runs Through

First, it was a boundary – in some sense
ours, our tape of un- and ever-changing
water music, our glitter-link fence....
Then it was up and sullen, disarranging

the edges of things. It was camped on the lawn.
Hadn't we seen the rag and plastic tidewrack
in the lower branches? We had been warned
and we still let it into our life. Now it falls back:

poor put-upon thing, it was trying to wash
itself clean, its tired towns, bringing nearly-new
hand-me-downs down like a gift, making lace

from landfill Tampax, wearing away, in its rush
to cope, its damaged banks, wearing what face
but our own? We are what it flows through.

Philip Gross's poetry collection, The Water Table, *won the TS Eliot Prize in 2009,* I Spy Pinhole Eye, *with photographer Simon Denison, won Wales Book of The Year 2010, and* Off Road To Everywhere *won the CLPE Award for Children's Poetry 2011.* Deep Field *(2011) and* Later *(2013) deal with ageing and language, seen through his father's aphasia. He has published ten novels for young people, and collaborated with artists, musicians, dancers and puppeteers. Two recent collaborations have centred on the river Taff – with film-maker Wyn Mason, creating the interactive poetry-film website,* Flow and Frame, *and currently with artist Valerie Coffin Price on the book,* A Fold In The River, *due from Seren, with accompanying exhibitions, in spring 2015. www.philipgross.co.uk*

PHOTO: STEVEN MORRIS

Philip Gross

WINNER CARDIFF INTERNATIONAL POETRY COMPETITION 2014

ISABEL ROGERS

John's Curious Machines

John Harrison (1693–1776) devoted his life to solving the 'longitude problem': to build a clock that can keep time in the humidity and motion at sea.

Adrift on dead reckoning, I hanged a sailor who warned me
the Scillies would rise in fog to drown two thousand men.
He swung for mutiny, gainsaying his Admiral, the day before I died.
I washed ashore wrung out with regret: not sucked down
by the black Atlantic with my fleet, but beached – killed
for my emerald ring – by a woman. She could have had my finger
but chose to leave no witness. John Harrison was then fifteen.

Thirty years on, *Centurion* fought a two-month ice storm,
ribboning her sails past Cape Horn. Each night scurvy culled
a man an hour. Ship and wind spent, she aimed blind
for Juan Fernandez along 35° South:
four days west, then back; two days east until Chile walled her in.
Turning again, the Commodore despaired. Half her crew
bled out below deck for want of her longitude.

John could not yet save them, conjuring seven hundred parts
for his 'curious third machine'. He hermited away two decades.
His first clock had sailed to Lisbon, horology pitched
against old ways of guesswork, calculation flaws
and half-blind sailors, their retina burned gauging lines
from moon to sun. His second's grasshopper escapement
trapped near-perfect time for no one. Men swore by the stars.

John believed in earthly time and vowed to coax it through his box.
Caged ball bearings rubbed out friction. One strip of brass and steel
broke the tyranny of temperature over gridiron pendula.
Twenty years to build! His third stood primed to pin ships on the sea,
but John forged those apprenticed years into a new wonder.
Barely two years on, his fourth was born: a jewelled miniature.
Rubies and diamonds rocked time quiet between them.

The *Deptford* bore it to Jamaica, counting crescent and gibbous moons
through half a year of pitch and toss, heat and rough weather.
John's son endured fevered sleep in The Watch's salty blankets
but- dry- it erred just two minutes. Still the Longitude Board
refused to pay. John's fifth and last went to the King. It proved
its forebears but stoked Maskelyne's fury: his jealous star-gazers
threw John's clocks on an unsprung cart and locked them up.

John died old, 7 minutes 35 seconds west of his chronometers.
They were forgot. Decades of sediment layered his precision;
rust and grease silting their geometry. Time nearly broke them.
A war-cracked man found their smudged intricacy;
mirrored their fragility. For twelve years he was patient
and healer, repaid by a slow synchronised return to motion.
Greenwich has them still, ticking out our time from the prime meridian.

***Isabel Rogers**' poetry has been published widely; she's currently working on a first collection. She also writes flash fiction and drama, and has just completed her second novel. isabelrogers.org. @Isabelwriter*

PATIENCE

JANE MACNAMEE LEARNS TO WALK AGAIN AFTER SURGERY

> Isn't it plain the sheets of moss, except that / they have no tongues, could lecture / all day if they wanted about // spiritual patience?
>
> Mary Oliver, 'Landscape', *New & Selected Poems*

PROOF OF LAND AS MEDICINE CAN BE FOUND IN THE VIEW FROM THE VAST three-paned window on the orthopaedic unit of Ysbyty Gwynedd, Bangor. I found myself there, aged thirty-eight, after years of surgery from childhood, some minor miracles, some utterly botched – waiting for a total hip replacement. I'd lived and walked in the hills and mountains of Wales for ten years and, I am ashamed to say, had not seen the sunrise over Snowdon consecutively for more than two days. That week, in a place where only the dead and comatose actually sleep, I was gifted with its vision every day, lilting a soft pink, and with it, left the overpowering smell of anaesthetic, urine and stale sweat behind and drifted off to sweeter tranquil places, to deep-rooted memories of walking those ridges without pain.

On the morning of the operation, the sunlight was so strong it reflected prismatic off that ancient rock face and flooded the ward with indigo and vermilion rays. At that moment I would have melted happily through the glass and been lost forever, but I lay there, leaden, grounded, stuck to the nylon fabric of my operating gown and the hot, cloying plastic of the hospital mattress, a disturbing shade of sickly, institutional green. Opposite me, Dot, who was waiting for a new knee, winked her encouragement. We'd become friends already and would be joined later by Val, also waiting for a new hip – the three of us brave, terrified and resigned, would wince and puke in trio, during the following few days.

A couple of hours before my trip to theatre, I received a visit from the anaesthetist, a tall, gaunt man, who perched corvid-like at the end of the bed. He asked me whether I would like to take the option of local rather than general anaesthetic. 'You are joking,' I responded. He smiled back serenely. 'No thanks,' I stuttered, 'I'd like the full works. And by the way, when do I get the pre-med?' The pre-med injection, I knew, from past experience, was the only sound way to get anyone with a slightly nervous disposition anywhere near an operating table. 'Oh, we don't do that anymore,' he told me. 'Don't worry, you'll be fine.' Breathe deeply, I thought, very deeply.

By mid-morning, I was on my way. In the process, I had to hand over my glasses. It was the moment of total surrender. Without my spectacles the whole world is impressionistic, people soften and flow beyond their edges, and I am caught between beauty and vulnerability. All I saw after their removal were the shiny smiley teeth of a lovely nurse who wheeled me towards theatre with soothing words and, on a wall in pre-op, the fuzzy silhouette in a photograph of a walker on top of the sunset peak of a ragged mountain. 'That's me,' I slurred, after a small scratch on the back of my hand when the drugs kicked in.

I woke up three hours later slightly too early, as they were lifting me out of what felt like some scaffolding arrangement, off the table. I opened my eyes and grinning wildly, opened my arms in an attempt to embrace the surgeon, who stood politely to one side. 'Thank you – thank you so much,' I started jabbering. 'They decided on ceramic in the end not metal,' I informed him and his assistants. 'It lasts longer apparently – it's my age, isn't it wonderful?' I gabbled all the way back to the ward, remembering one of the hospital porters asking, 'Have you just been for a run around the block, love?' Grin, grin, jabber. Ah yes, the joy, and thus of course, the restricted access to morphine. I pumped it into my bliss-filled veins at regulated intervals for the next three days, ready to face the end of the world if I had to.

Patience. Patient. *Patiens*. Lying there afterwards, I took suffering out of its meaning and focused on the waiting, the metamorphosis. I thought of myself first as a hibernating bear in deep winter, the body shut down, conserving energy, knowing the best course of action in a blizzard is to hunker down and curl up tight to keep the heat in. Then I was a caterpillar crawling on to a twig and starting to spin its chrysalis, wrapped in sheets of silk, the soft form inside mutating, melting, dissolving and new brilliant patterns emerging – wings.

On the outside, there was very little doing. I had to lie completely still to begin with, flat on my back with tubes travelling in and out of my body, drowning in the beeping of monitors and strapped to a black plastic wedge between my paralysed legs to stop me crossing them over. I couldn't feel my legs, only a heaviness, a sense of being packed in, bandaged and suffused in strange metallic smells. It was my body, but not mine. On the inside, drifting in and out of my dream world, there was a roar of movement, of morphine meditations. I was a flamenco dancer graced in fine sparkling red lace and black heels, with rapid rhythmic feet, I ran naked on a long glistening white beach, I screeched through the delicious scent of a bluebell wood, the soft sponge of moss springing me up to the cloudless sky. Inside, I had never been more lithe or alive.

Walking is how I have always found stillness in my mind, how I have stepped out of the edgy discord of too much human noise, back into harmony. Then, unable to walk, deep within in my pupa, I was exploring motion of a different, internal kind, and I didn't want to be moved by anyone on the outside. I wanted everything to knit back together, to find its own time to heal, but they insisted a day later that I had to go down to X-ray to check that all the bits and bobs, including the three-inch screw they had had to insert unexpectedly, were in place. I was scooped from bed to hospital trolley by stretcher howling 'F**k!' for which I apologised to the porters and especially to the nun at the end of the ward who was also in recovery. After that ordeal, which involved lying for a long time, helpless, on my trolley pinned against the wall of a busy corridor in the X-ray queue, I was transferred back to the ward and then Dave, the physio, appeared.

He seemed far too bullish and predatory for my liking – to which I responded, when he pulled my legs off the bed and tried to get me to stand only twenty-four hours after the operation, by vomiting my lunchtime tomato soup involuntarily all over him. Nesting fulmars (minus the soup) do the same to any predator approaching their small patch of cliff in an act of self-defence, projecting up to a metre, with lethal acidic consequences to their victims, whose wings become stuck and flightless. Dave would be fine. He just gave me a wide berth for a couple of days until they sent me someone else, who was much gentler. I did everything she told me.

In those first few days of having to move, Val and I lurched on seasick legs the huge distance of two feet between bed and armchair, whilst Dot's knee joint was painfully manipulated by a machine on the bed opposite. We laughed and cringed at our shared humiliations on the ward: the stale bread at breakfast; at senile Annie a few beds across from me who seemed convinced I had been her husband's lover and pointed her boney accusatory finger at me at regular intervals, hissing – 'You!' and then at gentler times, asked the nurses for pen, paper and stamps to write to me and 'sort all of this business out'; at the woman with long white hair and a billowing blue dressing gown, who had been in there so long she sat with the nurses at the staff station and got into any unoccupied bed whenever she fancied; at our naked humanity; our pathetic state; our stinking feet; the bare animal of us, and we dreamt of a bottle of wine with three straws to allievate the boredom.

A few days later, we were issued with crutches, pairs of clattering alien limbs, and all of us started walking, re-learning it, shuffling timidly, wary of our new bodies, trying to fit back in. Each day we went a little bit further. We progressed from a walk across the ward to the window, down the corridor, and then, the bold adventure to an open window overlooking the hospital car park. I cried as I drank it all in – the people below moving freely, the sweet smell of fresh air, the hills beyond. There was one final test before they let us out, to walk up and down a set of stairs without wobbling. I wobbled inside, I doubted, my legs felt so weak, and I lied. 'I'm fine,' I said, because I wanted out. The following morning, they released me.

Back home, my first steps outdoors felt so good on my skin, alive to the movement of air. Trapped in the stifling atmosphere of the hospital, my skin had been deadened, taut. Out, the elements awakened me again to the rawness of pure body, to the sense of touch. I remembered it all as if for the first time – the soft breeze of a late spring morning; the tang of salt on my lips at the shoreline; the fury of an autumn wind scarfing my hair around my cheeks; the scorch of sun walking through ice; the lying back in sand and tunneling my fingers deep into it, the heat soaking through skin to warm the pallor and the dankness of a long, sodden winter. The tingle of the air on that first afternoon was like being welcomed back into the arms of a loved one after a long, enforced separation, a cleaving in and never wanting to let go again. Touch – we humans, we were all born to touch. And now, I wanted to touch everything, to leap across the barriers on ancient monuments that said *Don't touch!* I wanted rock, the feeling of my hands moulding into it. I wanted the sharpness of gorse, the softness of moss, and the slime of earth. I wanted to touch the space between things.

With those early steps out, I was growing into the shape of my new body, wearing fresh scars on top of the old ones, learning the contours of a different landscape, the perceptible, and the ones I would keep hidden. Emerging, my wings were sticky. I took short daily walks, still with the crutches, along the pavement to a bench down the road to bask in the sun, and sat there for hours, listening to the wooden clunk of bowls on the green. For several days in a row, after sitting there for a while, a male blackbird would come and perch on the same cherry tree full of blossom in front of me and sing the most exquisite aria. On and on. I was enchanted by the layers and the texture of it, the transcendent power that came out of his small dark breast, wearing his history in that song as I wore mine now in this strange rejuvenating being, listening to familiar sounds with a keener ear. For a few weeks, that bench was my goal. After that, I would clack my way along Aberystwyth promenade and breathe the sea in deeply at an outdoor café, listening to the squeal of oystercatchers. I watched people stroll, skate and jog by. Soon, I would get rid of the crutches. Soon, I would walk on rough ground again. And then, slowly, slowly, mountain.

***Jane MacNamee** lives in Aberystwyth and writes on nature and the Welsh landscape.*

FRANCESCA RHYDDERCH PROFILES KOREAN AUTHOR LEE SEUNG-U

The Phenomenon of the Rain

BORN IN 1959, LEE SEUNG-U IS A LEADING NOVELIST OF KOREA. Throughout his career, Lee has meticulously explored the philosophical dimension of human existence. *In the Beginning, There Was the Temptation*, an adaptation of the Book of Genesis, reflects his interest in theological issues; his many works include *About Solar Eclipse, I Will Live Long,* and *A Help Wanted Ad. The Private Lives of Plants* has been translated into French and published under the title *La vie rêvée des plantes* by Gallimard. Another of his major novels, *The Reverse Side of Life,*[1] is published in English translation by Peter Owen. Lee is Professor of Creative Writing at Chosun University in South Korea.[2]

According to a statistic often quoted by those concerned about the future of literature in translation, only three per cent of books read in the UK have been translated into English from other languages, a figure which suggests – what, exactly? Resistance to literature outside the mainstream, to new writing from beyond the borders of our own culture, or simply a lack of intellectual curiosity? Literary journalist Boyd Tonkin, one of the founders and champions of the Independent Foreign Fiction Prize, argues that we need to look past this superficially depressing statistic at the complex publishing interface that lies behind it.[3] The attitude of UK publishers towards the business of translation varies, he says:

> *From those relatively few advocates and champions who have always been deeply committed, through to scepticism, indifference and outright hostility. Much of the hostility is not so much a principled antagonism towards translation, it's more a kind of laziness. That's because in order to make a work in translation effective in the British market all sorts of things have to happen, which is not the case in other kinds of fiction: the translation has to be commissioned, it has to be of an adequate quality and it has to be funded. Therefore as a publisher you need to know about things like the translation support available from embassies and cultural institutes. It also has to be marketed in a more intelligent and creative way than with a familiar homegrown name. And the author, in many cases, needs to be present and visible. This, as*

with publicity, creates its own logistical problems, especially if the author is not an English speaker. None of these are insuperable problems but they do require work, effort and forethought on behalf of publishers.

Fortunately for readers in Wales, the intelligent and creative work of the Wales Literature Exchange over the last fifteen years or so has done much to facilitate translation. The organisation's continued influence is evident in the perennially brave, commercially risky commissioning undertaken by leading Welsh publishers Seren and Parthian. Seren, for example, has recently announced their intention to purchase the English translation rights to *China 1957* by You Feng Wei, while Parthian is publishing English translations of Welsh-language novelist Wiliam Owen Roberts' *Petrograd* and Slovak writer Peter Krištúfek's *The House of the Deaf Man*. Working in close collaboration with Literature Across Frontiers, Wales Arts International and their partners worldwide, Wales Literature Exchange sends Welsh authors and their work out into the world, while also bringing writers from other countries to readers and audiences here. This is a reciprocal process which, among other things, makes an enormous contribution to the intellectual health of the Welsh readership. As Patrick McGuinness so eloquently put it at a recent symposium on Welsh and Chinese writing (organised by Wales Literature Exchange and Bangor University): 'Why should others be interested in our literature if we don't read the literature of others?'

Among the organisations with whom Wales Literature Exchange has a close alliance is the British Council, which earlier this year invited ten writers from Korea to participate in the London Book Fair and an associated series of satellite literary events across the UK. It was this diplomatically delicate venture that brought renowned Korean author Lee Seung-U to Aberystwyth in April, where he gave a public interview with me in the iconic Old College, assisted by translator Han Eui-Jong Karmy.

As we took our seats on a trio of wobbly bardic chairs in the Seddon Room, Han told me that Lee liked Aberystwyth already, because he had been born by the sea. I listened carefully to everything our translator told me in those few minutes before we got started: preparing for an interview with an author whose work has barely been translated into English is no easy task, and I knew that the translator's role in the session would be key. I was going to ask my questions in English and Lee Seung-U was going to answer in Korean. Han would translate each question (from English to Korean, for Lee's sake) and each answer (from Korean to English, for my sake, and that of the audience, bar a small group of Korean students), in a process perhaps best described as delayed, rather than simultaneous, translation. I warned our audience that despite their familiarity with translation between Welsh and English they might find this way of doing things a little unwieldy. However, Han was both a genuine fan of Lee Seung-U's work and an evidently able translator. She was the glue that held the evening together, managing to convey some of Lee Seung-U's character and humour beyond the bare bones of the answers that a more workmanlike translator might have offered us.

From the conversation that followed, it quickly emerged why the quietly spoken man sitting on the bardic chair next to me is a literary giant in his home country. Like all Koreans born since 1945, Lee has only ever known Korea as two countries rather than one, since it was divided into North and South Korea following the Second World War – a division along the 38th parallel which seemed relatively arbitrary at the time, but has since become a profoundly political line in the sand. As Claire Armitstead wrote in the *Guardian* recently, Korea remains a country 'sawn in half'.[4] North Korea, under Russian control, developed into a Communist state, while South Korea became and remains a pro-Western state. The authors brought to the UK this spring by the London Book Fair are – without exception and not surprisingly – from the South. We can only imagine the diplomacy that would be required to find a way into North Korea, whose political culture remains more or less closed to us in the West. (For those wanting to know more, the *Guardian*'s list of top ten books about North Korea[5] features titles by authors including defectors to South Korea and a former Beijing Reuters correspondent.)

Lee Seung-U was one of the generation of South Korean writers to emerge after the political repression of the 1980s, and he was immediately spotted as a literary star of the future by the judges of the New Writer's Award. He has since garnered many more accolades and prizes, and has published numerous novels and short story collections, including *The Reverse Side of Life*: when the English translation of this title appeared in 2005, it finally established Lee internationally as a serious philosophical novelist. However, the thirteen-year delay between the publication of *The Reverse Side of Life* in Korean in 1992 and its translation into English indicates another hurdle faced by readers of work in translation. By the time a book is available to a broader international readership, the author may have long since moved on to different ways of writing and perhaps different topics. In the case of Lee Seung-U, though, whose abiding interest is in the connections between the spiritual and the secular, the everyday and the mystical as well as the mythical, his engagement is overridingly with the human condition. *The Reverse Side of Life* therefore seems as fair a starting-point as any for a discussion of his work.

One of the most striking aspects of this book is its form. If such a complex philosophical and self-reflexive novel can be summarised at all, it is perhaps best to say simply that it has two main characters and that both these characters are writers. They are also both narrators in an oblique sense, in that the primary narrator, who has been briefed to research and write about the main character, Bak Bugil, transcribes and quotes from large swathes of quotations from stories and novels by Bugil himself, in addition to secondary sources about him and his work, such as critical articles and interviews. The effect is one that will be familiar to readers of postmodern novels. A few pages in and you think you know what to expect: a structurally ambitious, difficult novel which will keep your emotions in check while plumbing the depths of your philosophical consciousness. But the most surprising and perhaps exciting aspect of this book is that it is a postmodern novel which succeeds in carrying the reader along with the main characters while encouraging us to reflect on the construction of the novel itself. This is ultimately a novel about the heart as much as the head. 'There are skills in love, too,' we are told. 'If one needs to learn and practise the skills needed to live, it should be all the more so for love. This is because there is nothing more precious and valuable than love.'

Despite its many disparate elements, *The Reverse Side of Life* is therefore an organic whole, moving seamlessly from one 'source' to another. The novel's success in this respect is due to the impact made by the various texts on the narrator-character himself – perhaps he is a 'reverse side' of Bak Bugil and even of Lee Seung-U. His is no dry, academic voice: he is always responding rather than analysing or even riffing for stylistic effect. In short, he is constantly alive in his own made, unmade and remade text.

Other authors among the ten brought over from Korea to the UK for the London Book Fair have spoken in interviews about the need to teach the younger generation in Korea about the history and politics of their own divided country. I couldn't help but think of this division when I was reading *The Reverse Side of Life*: I wondered, could the splintered narration – and indeed the fractured postmodern text itself – somehow be traced back to the split identity of Korea? Does the personal have a political bearing in Lee's work? When I put this question to him, he answered it with all the seriousness that he had accorded me throughout our discussion, but it was clear that he thinks of himself first and foremost as a writer, and not a Korean writer. His critics can think about politics if they so wish, but he thinks only about his work. The primary object of his enquiry is the human condition – our day-to-day existence and how it relates to the spiritual. *The Reverse Side of Life* is no political manifesto: if it is a handbook at all it is one for how we are to live, in which the simplest questions can also be the most complex, as is shown in this brief meditation on dual perspectives:

> *Of course, any two people may give different weight to the same thing. Take the story of the umbrella seller and the straw-sandal seller. The happiness and unhappiness of the two are diametrically opposed to one another, dependent on one fact (rain). When one of them is happy, the other is unhappy. For this reason, one person owes their happiness to another's unhappiness. Therefore, it is not right for the umbrella seller to ask why the straw-sandal seller is unhappy when he himself is happy, nor conversely for the straw-sandal seller to ask why the umbrella seller is crying*

> *when he himself is laughing. Nevertheless, the two are alike in that their expectations and disappointments are entirely based on the phenomenon of the rain. The weather determines whether or not they are happy. Whether or not it rains is a serious matter.*

It comes as no surprise to learn that Lee studied theology, graduating from Seoul Theological University and Yonsei University Graduate School of Theology. His first novel, *A Portrait of Erysichton*, was initially conceived as a response to the attempted assassination of Pope John Paul in 1981, a fact which is often quoted in the few English-language articles about his work. It was evident from our conversation that he is frequently asked about the influence of religion on his writing, and he clearly feels that this question is something of a red herring. He doesn't understand it, he told me, when people ask him why he went on to become a novelist after studying theology. People train in all kinds of fields and progress through all walks of life before becoming writers. That's what gives them their humanity. As our interview drew to a close he put his own question to our appreciative, evidently reflective, audience: why *not* study theology and then become a novelist? Perhaps there is no better subject to study before becoming a novelist in order to understand the depths of human endeavour and our attempts to rationalise the significance (or otherwise) of our lives. 'A novel,' as he has said elsewhere, 'is neither the writer's intention, nor the subject, but an expression of existence.'

Francesca Rhydderch*'s debut novel,* The Rice Paper Diaries, *was longlisted for the Authors' Club Best First Novel Award and won the fiction category of the Wales Book of the Year Award. She is currently working on a collection of short stories.*

[1] Lee Seung-U, *The Reverse Side of Life* (Peter Owen, 2005).
[2] literature.britishcouncil.org/projects/2014/london-book-fair-2014/a-lee-seung-u
[3] prohelvetia.ch/Interview.1566.0.html?&L=2
[4] theguardian.com/books/2014/apr/07/inside-story-korea-london-book-fair
[5] theguardian.com/world/2014/may/29/the-best-books-on-north-korea

PAULA BOHINCE

The Cheese Shop

Incandescent, I could be a Master's
subject: local, in housedress. Palm outstretched,
stopped by an invisible force,
shamed but luminous by these imports. Here
is writ the memoir of cattle
huddled on lavender'ed hillsides, like black
revolving roses. Here the story of green-eyed
goats who leapt in wooden shoes.

Stilton ribboned with raspberries; red-
dressed Gouda; Feta abandoning strength, crumbling
like islands into the ocean; Port
blushed as a sunset; blonde
Cheddar of Vermont made exotic, stoic as Frost
as he scowled at the mountains and wrestled
with angels, aiming to remain upright, writing and
writing, as one by one his children died.

From Mother's breast I hardened,
was weaned and wept in my crib. Salt-drenched,
exhausting the darkness. Little
calf, I leaned between bars to watch the farmer
at dawn, a Veronica, wiping the face
of the newborn, who shivered on weak legs. Steam
from the labour burned off their skins, as from
a tin pail when the hot milk hits it.

How the eye will flutter over notes of cream,
aged yellows, Delft blue that runs through some
like a body streaked with cancer.
In this maternal corner are everywhere Mother's wet
cheeks at my wedding, shining
with each morsel: four guests and four courses,
and the servants' kind stories, explaining each one's
pretty origin, to his poor and my poor.

Bluebird

Of happiness: I knew it
once. In the blue eye of a white horse
a neighbour kept,

that answered to the lowliest
signal. Walked a childhood's length
toward me. Not mine,

though the childhood was, entirely.
No mistake. The eye a blue bell
rung with animal kindness,

blue as the fatal instinct
children have. To go willingly toward
whatever hand opens.

In the blue air above me,
that blue eye. Still as a jay on a bough
you mourn already.

Gray fretwork, a barn, air a bonfire
dwindling. The horse in such
vapour unrivalled by another,

though I did not know what it meant
to compete. A pony going sway. Birch
white against birch trees.

Paula Bohince *is the author of* The Children *and* Incident at the Edge of Bayonet Woods. *She received second prize in the 2013 UK National Poetry Competition.*

BRUCE BOND

The Paintings of the Chauvet Cave

Time was a man laid his hunted down
in a cave like this, cut open the fresh

steam of the body, and began to paint.
Look around. No human figures here.

Only horses, lions, a chimera, an owl.
Each an avatar, or so they would be,

each an infant hour we can't recall,
we who crawl on all fours to enter.

And for what. To breathe the inner chamber,
hear the voices that are no longer ours,

echoes that shatter bat-like into silence.
If what you see are echoes, you are an echo's

echo, one more bison with all eight legs
caught in the stampede of the singular.

Time was a man wanted to be two,
four, eight such men, that, in the middle

of the night, longed to be one again.
Night bore down with its axe in the woods,

and the trees became a wilderness.
Ask the girl in convalescence who opens

a box of paints and feels a little better.
The same storm interrogates her window.

The same scavenger crawls from the hills.
The girl knows. When a hand lays a face

on death, it is not death. Only a face.
Not the beast of discouragement,

but the part that lives as the beast goes down.
These imitations, they begin in something.

These echoes return in a stranger voice.
Be calm, it says. Be watchful at the threshold.

Be thankful as the slaughtered shadows fall,
west to east, over the blood-stained wall.

***Bruce Bond** is the author of nine published books of poetry, most recently* Choir of the Wells: A Tetralogy *(Etruscan, 2013),* The Visible *(LSU, 2012),* Peal *(Etruscan, 2009), and* Blind Rain *(LSU, 2008). In addition he has three books forthcoming:* The Other Sky *(poems in collaboration with the painter Aron Wiesenfeld, Etruscan Press),* For the Lost Cathedral *(LSU Press), and a book of critical essays,* Immanent Distance: Poetry and the Metaphysics of the Near at Hand *(University of Michigan Press). Presently he is a Regents Professor of English at the University of North Texas and Poetry Editor for* American Literary Review.

The Hares I Have Seen

The first crashed a fence in a field near Shrewsbury.
It was after lunch of lamb slow-roasted for a night
and a day, its grease still slick on my fingers when she broke
from the stubble. I forgot her later when I sat on a swing
and cried. That time it was for loneliness.

The second raced the train taking me to Edinburgh.
A break in the hedge revealed for a blink the reach
of her stride, the gathering of feet beneath belly before
the hedge snapped back. I forgot her later when I cried
into moussaka. That time it was for loneliness and drink.

The third hung from a hook in a butcher's in Ludlow.
Her legs were primly crossed and bound, her head
shrouded in muslin but there was no mistaking
the checked spring, the white flag beneath her tail.
She was too big that close though her ears were shorn
because what good are ears when paying by weight?
I couldn't forget her but by then I'd given up crying.

That night she was in the mirror. She pulled off the muslin
to parade her holed skull, rolled her pale eyes and – worst of all –
flashed a stiff grin of yellow teeth bared to chip any dish
I'd try to jug her in. I went to bed without flossing. I cried
into my own dry fur. That time it was for everything.

***Katherine Stansfield** is a poet, fiction writer and reviewer. Her first book of poems,* Playing House, *is published by Seren this autumn. Her first novel,* The Visitor, *was published by Parthian in 2013. She lives in Aberystwyth. katherinestansfield.blogspot.co.uk/*

REVIEWS

The BAD DOCTOR
THE TROUBLED LIFE AND TIMES OF DR IWAN JAMES
'Comics from the dark side of medicine...speaks brilliantly and honestly'
BMJ Medical Humanities
IAN WILLIAMS

The Bad Doctor: The Troubled Life & Times of Dr Iwan James Ian Williams

Myriad Editions £12.99, PB, ISBN 9781908434289

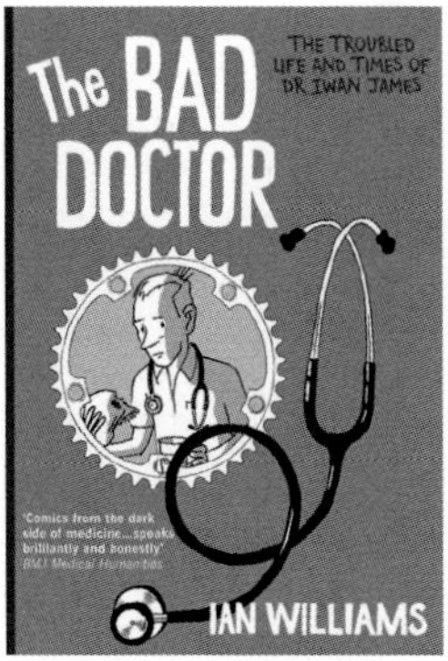

Ellen Bell assesses a graphic novel offering catharsis to jaded medics, and enjoys encounters with an amateur taxidermist, a syphilitic JP and Dr Iwan's OCD

After training as a doctor, Ian Williams honed his drawing skills at art school and in 2007, while working as a general practitioner in rural Wales, he began publishing strip cartoons on his website, www.graphicmedicine.org under the pseudonym Thom Ferrier. *The Bad Doctor: The Troubled Life and Times of Dr Iwan James* is his first graphic novel.

Comics such as *The Beano*, with their irreverent narratives and anarchic characters, were long considered to be the sole preserve of children. Trashy, easy reads frowned upon by adults, they were bought with pocket money and consumed as greedily and as quickly as ten penn'orth of sweets. Parents, teachers, neighbours and siblings, none were spared the lampooning and the more preposterous the scenario the better. Here was a safe space to represent, contain and work through all that pre-adolescent angst. Ian William's graphic novel, *The Bad Doctor*, appears to offer that same catharsis but to grown-up, jaded medics.

The Bad Doctor narrates the trials and tribulations of Dr Iwan, a middle-aged, conscience-ridden GP. There are his daily, often perplexing, encounters with his various patients such as Aneurin Cotter, the dark-glasses-wearing amateur taxidermist, Mr Roberts, the syphilitic Justice of the Peace and Julie with her borderline personality disorder. The book maps his relationship with his wife Carole and with his fellow doctors, Lois (for whom he is clearly nursing a crush) and Robert, the pugnacious senior partner. Outside of surgery hours he cycles, meeting up with his gay friend, Arthur.

'A graphic novel is like a film,' says the cartoonist Posy Simmonds, 'there are close-ups and long shots. You choose the location… and you get the characters to act.' In *The Bad Doctor*, Williams certainly exploits the graphic novel's cinematic potential, deftly revealing the underlying theme of Dr Iwan's unresolved childhood neuroses through flashbacks and chiaroscuro, and panning in and out from the claustrophobic, utilitarian-ness of the surgery to the wide stretch of the Welsh landscape. The passage of time is cleverly represented by objects that reflect Dr Iwan's current state of mind such as the Grim Reaper's scythe, a crucifix, a cycle gear, an egg-timer and the wheel of Fortune tarot card.

By aping the fast-moving, linear style of children's comics and the classic B-movie, the graphic novel (a phrase first coined in the mid-1960s) is able to explore the serious side of life in an easy, almost flippant way. As Williams says, 'We know the rules... we can also flip a few panels ahead... like fast-forwarding... a DVD.' Stunning examples such as Art Speigelman's *Maus* spring to mind, a moving depiction of the Holocaust, where Jews are mice, Germans are cats and non-Jewish Poles are pigs, as does Raymond Briggs' *When the Wind Blows*, a poignant portrayal of a nuclear attack, seen through the eyes of pensioners, Jim and Hilda Bloggs. *The Bad Doctor*, with its compassionate rendition of Dr Iwan's OCD (such as when as a child he had to say goodnight to all his toys and teddies in a particular order) has some of their pathos but lacks their depth and beauty. The drawings of his bike-rides against the sweep of the countryside are nicely observed but all too often the characters are not made distinct enough and the light and shade, both graphic and implied, lacks real contrast.

Nevertheless, as an antidote to the stresses and strains of modern life where the medical profession is still expected to cure all, *The Bad Doctor* is a warm, witty and undemanding read and Dr Iwan, with his self-doubt, superstitions and occasional profanity, is a well-observed and engaging Everyman.

***Ellen Bell** is an artist and writer currently living in Aberystwyth.*

Ugly Bus Mike Thomas

William Heinemann, £14.99, HB, ISBN 9780434022595

For **Chris Moss** this Cardiff-set crime novel by an ex-cop rings true, offering something akin to a new brand of working-class fiction bridging the televisual and the literary

Somewhere between the romanticised detective fictions of Ian Rankin and Colin Dexter and the depressing reality of gritty, formulaic television documentaries about speeding motorists and midnight drunks lies the shadowy world of real police work.

Mike Thomas worked for two decades as a cop before turning to novel writing, and his working-class characters, down-at-heel urban locations and hard-boiled language ring true. Much of the dialogue in *Ugly Bus* is delivered in a dry slang that can become wearing at times but is probably true to form. The title is typical, the 'ugly bus' referring to the TSG or Territorial Support Group police vans that patrol our city centres, especially on special events and Saturday nights. Five cops (Martin, Flub, Dullas, Vince, Flinch) have been assigned said vehicle for the Boxing Day football derby. As well as the inevitable stresses of coping with drunken, raucous, potentially violent fans, the cops have to keep apart two groups of political activists. Damned by one faction as 'Nazi scum' and by the other as allies of the Unite Against Fascism protestors, they are obliged to remain publically neutral while reflecting on their own individual prejudices.

The fact that the sergeant in charge, Martin Finch, is younger than the rest of the crew generates its own tensions. The trope of the naïve but idealistic head cop is hardly new, but by throwing his man into an environment that requires split-second decision-making in the company of four case-hardened veterans, Thomas ensures we're kept well away from the clichés of macho confrontation so familiar from American films. Instead the cooped-up men are watchful and mistrusting, but ultimately compelled to guide and support one another while keeping up fronts.

Good fiction sometimes has a claustrophobic quality, pulling the reader into its world and staying there for the duration. Whether we're flashing back to relevant episodes in each of the cops' lives or playing Bullshit Bingo to while away the time, throughout *Ugly Bus* we're kept very close to these five men at all times. A sweaty, hormonal intimacy evolves that is unpleasant –

these men are pretty hard to like – even if we enjoy a fly-on-the-wall angle on the life of ordinary policemen. Theirs is a world of acronyms, codewords, nicknames, insults and inside jokes, at once unremittingly mediocre and repellent – anyone still harbouring any nostalgic notions of neighbourhood plods and nice young men in smart uniforms will find them dashed here.

A long shift in the TSG van has the effect of turning the outside world into a sort of stage-set. While Cardiff is namechecked throughout *Ugly Bus*, the city feels vague and imprecise. There is little in Thomas' descriptions of streets and civic spaces that appeals to the senses. Like his widely praised debut, *Pocket Notebook*, this follow-up – which features one of the characters from the earlier novel – focuses narrowly on the worlds of work and the grimness of ordinary life for ordinary people. The mantra of the operation, 'What happens on the van stays on the van', captures the moral and imaginative limitations of the world the five cops inhabit.

The fact that the five cops are men wouldn't necessarily put off female readers, but there is something lewd and laddish about many of the descriptions of women. In any case, the only women in this book are offstage wives and girlfriends and one young woman who eventually – and dramatically – moves to the centre of the story as it unfolds. Sometimes the prose descends into a sort of Carry On up the Force pastiche ('His wife Sandra was a ripe and volatile brunette... her plentiful breasts regularly and pleasingly separated by the shaft of the Brains beer pump'), and sex is almost always couched in terms that are either performance-related – intercourse is 'pistoning' – or just plain sexist.

Yet for all this, the men in *Ugly Bus* are not quite two-dimensional. All the throwaway words and thoughts, the gags and brash exchanges, are framed by inner lives. Thomas shows the reader that while a certain hardness on the surface is the way policemen get through a day's work, there are expanses of boredom too in which each man reflects on his own predicament. In this respect, he is perhaps striving to offer the reader something akin to a new brand of working-class fiction, which bridges the televisual and the literary.

The problem with *Ugly Bus*, though, is ultimately basic: who is this novel for? It lacks the verve and cheek of Sixties novels about working men but also lacks the linguistic energy of contemporary writers such as Irvine Welsh or the social conscience of Chris Cleave. While the dramas inside the van and inside each cop's head are as febrile as those out on the streets and the terraces, they never quite rise above the category of occupational hazards. By making his Cardiff neutral, Thomas may have hoped to reach out to readers from beyond his geographical milieu, but *Ugly Bus* will probably be most popular with those who work within its narrow moral horizons – that is, fellow policemen. This is a tribute to its accuracy and authenticity, but also a reflection of its shortcomings.

Dark Actors: The Life and Death of Dr David Kelly
Robert Lewis

Simon & Schuster, £8.99, PB, ISBN 9780857209184

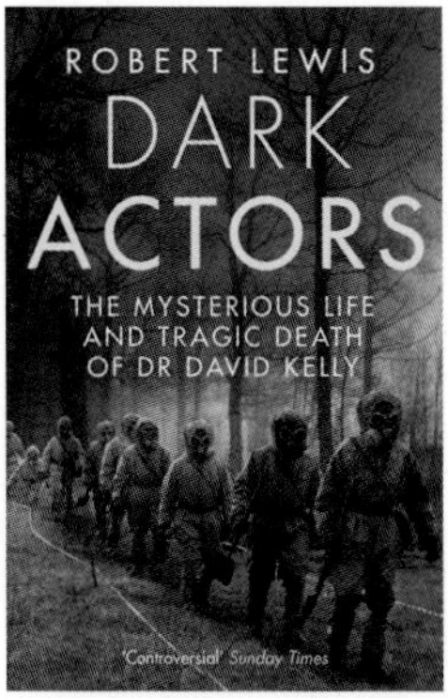

How did a quiet young Rhondda scientist join the dark actors of war games? **Chris Moss** admires this gripping and formidable book's attempts to find out

The death of weapons inspector Dr David Kelly on 17 July 2003 was one of several shadowy episodes surrounding British and allied military intervention in Saddam Hussein's Iraq. Because of the time-sensitive, shock-hungry nature of rolling news coverage, the mystery – and tragedy – of his alleged suicide was soon lost in a blur of surrounding detail, most notably the commissioning and composition of the so-called 'dodgy dossier' that helped justify the US-led invasion on 19 March and the controversy surrounding BBC reporter Andrew Gilligan's claim that the dossier had been 'sexed up' by the government.

Rhondda-born Kelly was not the kind of man we're used to seeing on the teatime news. As a bacteriologist, virologist and career civil servant, he spent almost all of his life far from the flashlights of the global media. Lewis struggles to find anything of special relevance in the first thirty years of his life, except perhaps that success in the world of science allowed Kelly to reinvent himself. Bereft of one parent and estranged from another, and short of any serious friends, Kelly was an ideal candidate to work in areas such as defence and biological weapons; without quite saying that you have to be rootless to join the 'dark actors' engaged in such affairs, Lewis suggests that it probably helps.

The wider world into which the gifted young scientist is thrust is fascinating at several levels – most particularly where chemistry, arms and politics collide – and Lewis tells a gripping story with many twists. Along the way we find out about a number of technicians and employees in the chemicals business in post-apartheid South Africa who disappeared or died. We wander down the labyrinthine corridors and into the locked labs of Porton Down in Wiltshire, the home of the UK's secretive chemical warfare and defence research facilities for almost a century. We meet a Soviet scientist who reveals to MI6 and DIS that Moscow is exploring ways to use cruise missiles to spray the West with an aerosolised bacterium called *Yersinia pestis* – better known as black death. We discover that invisible fatal chemicals have long been on the agenda of state intelligence departments.

Lewis has done a formidable job in linking David Kelly directly and indirectly to faraway places and past events, and *Dark Actors* provides us with a fascinating peek into the remote world of weapons development and inspection. Those who lived through the media coverage of the 1990–91 Gulf War will be reminded how the propaganda and lies started early on, how we were stirred into awe about Iraq's 'elite Republican Guard' and primed for an American invasion. The sections of the narrative that deal with Kelly remind us that for those on the ground, WMDs were not a spectre but a job of work, tools to be managed and governed. A portrait of a quiet, inquisitive, keen-eyed scientist emerges – a man extremely useful to the British government for gathering information and know-how, but only up to the point where realpolitik must take over.

When it comes to reconstructing the events surrounding Kelly's death, Lewis is unable to penetrate much further than journalists following the story at the time. All kinds of theories have been offered to explain Kelly's alleged suicide: that he was 'unreliable and eccentric'; that he was a deluded Walter Mitty; that he was a lovestruck romantic failure; that he was depressed and remorseful after talking to the press and losing his security clearance and all the status that went with it. But by the end, Lewis and we the readers are none the wiser as to the true cause. As we are told early on in the book, 'When New Labour finally fell from power, the incoming Conservative government resisted the mounting legal pressure to hold a proper inquest into Kelly's death by releasing the post-mortem reports instead.'

Lewis confesses, at the close of the book, to feeling a sort of calm after attempting to at least contextualise the death of Dr David Kelly. The writing of history mirrors media reportage in that it links causes and effects in such a way that the death of one man is not recorded as a singular tragedy but merely as one in a cycle of events. But history has the advantage of not needing to make headlines, and Lewis has served it by providing a highly detailed account of the hundreds of small, seemingly inconsequential movements and discreet messages and faceless men, and women, that surround the sad passing of a civil servant. In this respect he has done a good deal more than the Hutton Inquiry, which is shown up to be a wholly partial, even corrupt, attempt at extending the cover-up. But Lewis reminds us that to join the 'dark actors' in their war games, even at a superficially low, technical level and in a non-public capacity, always involves a degree of risk and collusion. Kelly, in the wider setting of New Labour's Machiavellian operations, was a fall guy – and those who used him and then survived him are free to go on spreading the half-truths and untruths. If David Kelly killed himself, many have blood on their hands; if he was murdered, they have more blood on their hands. But their hands are drenched in any case.

Chris Moss *is a travel writer living in Laugharne.*

The North (And Almost Everything In It) Paul Morley

Bloomsbury, £10.99, PB, ISBN 9781408834015

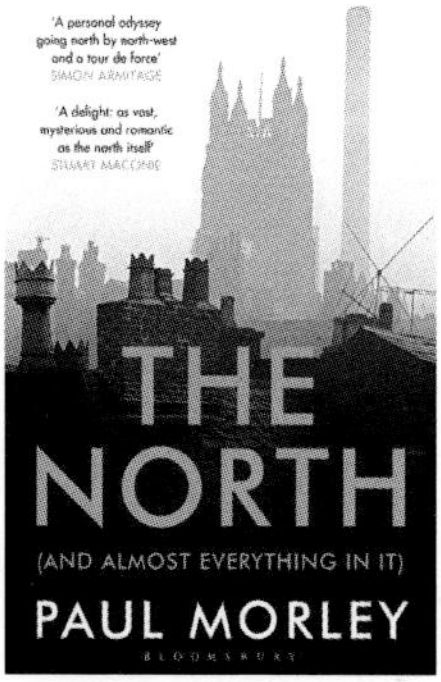

On the eve of the Scottish independence referendum, this 'cut and paste' job, for **Ted Parry,** singularly fluffs the opportunity to offer the north of England a unifying myth

Some books are best judged by their cover. This one is a monochrome of mist, TV aerials, church and chimneystacks. The title is similarly revealing. That bracket looks boastful but 'almost' is another word for failure. The failure's nature is suggested by poet Simon Armitage's strapline, 'A personal odyssey'.

Morley flashes this personal poetic licence even at his own life, unilaterally declaring history:

> *For the sake of this book – estimating, assuming, inventing, elaborating and consolidating in the ways that history most often gets written – I have decided that the exact day I arrived in Reddish... was the day the Beatles played their one and only gig in Stockport.*

Meaning it's OK to make it up – that's what everybody else does. But it's not. They don't.

Instead of references:

> *If there was to be a series of bracketed academic numbers attached to these facts, dates, quotes and traces, the straightforward explanation of their source would be that they were found on the World Wide Web, and then framed, filtered and spun until they fitted into my story of the north.*

This denies credit to real researchers. One example: obscure details of the opening chord to 'A Hard Day's' Night' are dropped into a literary lobscouse stirred with the word 'Liverpool'. I recognised the source. For generations of guitarists, that chord was the Holy Grail. In Dominic Pedler's *Songwriting Secrets of the Beatles*, a great intellect seized it. Morley could have said 'Thanks'.

THE NORTH's capitalisation within the book, likewise, is anti-intellectual. It saves debating if this is '*the* north *of* England', or *a* 'North' meaning something else. When the issue is unavoidable, the action jumps elsewhere. George Harrison is quoted saying The Beatles' accent is 'not English, it's Liverpudlian'. My eyes flicked forward for a discussion of what it might mean to be English – or not. Instead, we get the Stones in Rochdale.

In place of analysis, Morley wanders, like a bad poet, through meaningless moorlands of sparse verbs:

> *The north of England, with England being north-west of Europe, and Europe being in the northern hemisphere, and north being a word that says so much and leaves plenty to the imagination... existing below Scotland, which is another north altogether.*

Or: 'No other north but this north, inside and outside England, which consists of this fluid, static piece of land, this....'

He also swerves around the north–south divide. It's just a 'standardised national story'. But if it's true, then no national story exists. At least, not one about 'England'. If it isn't, there's no justification for a book about the north. Here we find the consistent logic behind Morley's omissions.

In the 1980s, industries across north England, Wales and Scotland were destroyed, targeting working-class organisation and culture. That included the 1984–5 Miners' Strike. Nobody who lived through it forgot. Except Paul Morley. During these years too were bitter, deeply contrasting, football disasters of Heysel and Hillsborough – with the fallout from the latter finally proving deep calumny throughout the English establishment. Despite ongoing working-class demoralisation, Oasis and Pulp made the North and 'Common People' central to popular culture in the 1990s, soon after the Poll Tax turned Thatcher toxic. That cultural shift ushered in Labour's 1997 landslide. Tony Blair, Labour leader (and northern MP) kidded himself and the commentariat that it was because the Labour Party rebranded, rather than because the electorate went Left. All this is absent from Morley's world.

This was also the era when Scotland and Wales reorganised oppositional politics and culture. Civic nationalism negotiated with working-class socialism, language activism, the anti-nuclear movement, feminism and gender identities, environmentalism, community campaigns and anti-racism. Consequently the Scots are now close to leaving the 'United' Kingdom that their nobles dragged them into three centuries back. If Scotland finds the courage, Wales will follow. If she does not, the gleeful 'austerity' of the City of London and its three right wings at Westminster will be horrific – just like after 1979. But the region that will suffer most from a Scots 'No' will be the North.

No regional assembly, parliament, party or army stands between it and the permanent counter-revolution. No flags fly. No single accent sounds. No patron saints offer blessings. No myth unifies. No maps mark imagined frontiers. Most of all, no art, imagination or intellect – with the magnificent exception of the *Angel of the North* – act yet to glue this possible nation, twice as populous as Scotland, equal in historical achievement to anywhere on Earth, together before the coming plague.

That's what I sought: a two-hundred ton literary sculpture equal to its subject. I wanted too much. But nobody deserved an ex-northerner, stuck in the seventies, cutting, pasting, googling and making it up at a London desk. And missing out everything the old story said he would.

Ted Parry *is a Liverpudlian by birth, a Fenlander by upbringing, and a Welsh socialist by adoption and inclination. He plays music, with occasional diversions into print and political activism as a result of inspiration or conscience.*

My Family and Other Superheroes Jonathan Edwards

Seren, PB, £19.99, ISBN 9781781721629

João Morais finds it impossible to dislike these warm, moving and confessional poems about family, warts an' all

My Family and Other Superheroes. It might sound like something penned by Simon Armitage, but this moving array of poems about family and experience could only have been written by Jonathan Edwards. I must state a bold claim at the beginning of this review, no matter how stupid it might sound: it is impossible to dislike this collection. It's a portrayal of family and Valleys life written without judgement. It doesn't matter, for instance, that the poet's father's 'filming dates' aren't quite the same as Google's on meeting Sophia Loren at Crumlin Viaduct. What comes through more than anything is the warmth and affection Edwards feels towards his family.

And it is Jonathan Edwards and his own family, with all their fault-lines and quirks, that the majority of the poems are about. There is no narrator with a capital N here. This is highly confessional stuff, warts and all if you will – and it is all the better for it.

The lived experience of the collection's main subject is its main strength but also its greatest weakness. Edwards has perfected the art of tugging at the heartstrings. Despite the evident poignancy of these individual pieces, the feel of a distinct yet repeated pattern emerges after reading half a dozen: Edwards describes a light-hearted scene in which he or a member of his family interacts with some brand of popular culture (whether it be a person or an event), where at the crucial moment we are reminded that this happened in the past, giving an extra level of meaning to the scene, both in a nostalgic and touching way.

It does of course work every time, but such a structure, once spotted, is hard to forget. In 'Half Time, Wales vs Germany, Cardiff Arms Park, 1991', we're talked through the changing room happenings of a celebrated Welsh national football side. Ratcliffe, Sparky, Big Nev and Giggs are forty-five minutes away from creating history by beating the world champions. Everyone is nervous, especially the eventual match winner, Ian Rush. But 'what he doesn't know / is I'm in the stand in my father's coat, / storing things to tell at school the next day.' Can you not help but love these lines? What is more important to Edwards is who he's sharing the experience with and how it has undoubtedly shaped the man he has become today. But having read a notable number of similar poems, it's possible to tell exactly which way the last third of the poem will go.

Elsewhere the poems take on a political slant, showing a distinctly (Welsh) anti-establishment leaning. 'In John F Kennedy Airport' tells the story of a Wales that 'no longer exists', a country that has been replaced with a 'small museum in Kansas' where the Welsh experience has been recreated – one of Male Voice Choirs and Tom Jones and every other nauseous done-to-death stereotype of the last ever. The citizens of the former nation are all in mourning, except for one establishment figure, who 'danced a jig, laughing' at this news as his own condition in life is improved as a result.

'The Performance' takes a darker turn again. 'On a quiet Tuesday in our village,' it starts, 'workmen started putting up a stage in the square.' These workers 'spoke no English'. When no one turns up to take to it, the villagers eventually get drunk and start fighting until it collapses. The workers, 'speaking no English', return to find their handiwork undone.

You've no doubt noticed I mentioned the two pivotal lines about the workmen's language. Maybe it's because I'm bored that language is still a contentious issue in twenty-first century Wales, or maybe it's because I'm forcing it to be in this poem. It would after all be easy to read that repetitious variant of 'speaking no English' as being comparable to 'siarad yn Gymraeg', especially if one were to read the empty stage brought in by outsiders as something akin to the Senedd. But 'speak no English' could just as easily mean 'not speak my language', which is something the political classes find exceedingly easy to do when it comes to conversing with the rest of us. Either way, the political poems show Edwards as a staunch defender of his people, showing as much empathy and emotional passion to the community in which he grew up as he does to those closest to him.

João Morais *is studying for a PhD in Creative Writing at Cardiff University. A nominee for the 2009 Rhys Davies Short Story Competition, he won the Terry Hetherington Award in 2013. His work appears in* Nu2: Memorable Firsts, *amongst other publications.*

Water Lloyd Jones (trans Lloyd Jones)

Y Lolfa, £8.95, PB, ISBN 9781847718181

While **Angharad Penrhyn Jones** urges authors to explore the problems of climate change within a Welsh context, for her this novel beats the drum of protest at the expense of structure, viewpoint and characterisation

Lloyd Jones' third novel, originally published in Welsh, examines the catastrophic impacts of climate change on the physical environment and the traditional way of life in rural Wales. Known best for his epic, fantastical travelogue-style novels, Jones has now ventured into darker territory, one which is often ignored by literary writers. This is also his first attempt at a conventionally plotted novel. It's a courageous move.

Water portrays life on an upland farm in north Wales at an unspecified time in the future. The family members have left the lawless and dangerous cities of Britain and returned to their original home. Conditions are harsh: the seasons are unpredictable and food is scarce. With water moving into the basin of the valley, the family becomes increasingly isolated and no longer has access to medicine or electricity. The old man of the house, Wil, obsessively tends to his chickens while he loses both his physical strength and his grip on the world. His daughter Elin has taken to her bed, where she reads fashion magazines: she, too, is retreating into fantasy. His grandchildren lack basic subsistence skills: Huw has to be taught how to catch a fish and Mary struggles to bake a cake. It's a bleak scenario indeed, and a sense of claustrophobia pervades the novel. But the arrival of a Polish man with impressive survival skills brings some hope of change.

The setting feels authentic: Jones writes with authority about the struggle to rear animals and grow crops at a time when natural processes have gone awry. Yet the world and the characters he conjures up never really spring to life. This is partly a problem of perspective: the constant and rather arbitrary shifts in narrative point of view make it difficult to get under the skin of any one character. That we know almost nothing about their backstory, at least until later chapters, doesn't help.

But it is also a problem of language. The slaughtering of a pig is rendered thus: 'In the next couple of hours he chopped up the pork into half a dozen sections.' One can imagine a writer like Cynan Jones capturing the physicality of such a scene in all its visceral horror; *Water*, however, is oddly sterile, even coy. When a baby is born to a key character, we remain distanced from the event. The author chooses not to dwell on a decomposing body or the problems of disposing of human excrement. He tells us his characters are living a debased and 'primitive' existence – they are 'like animals in the wild' – but when it comes to describing the texture of this existence, Jones is squeamish, and often relies on well-worn phrases whose impact is weak.

Moreover, the temporal element of the story doesn't entirely convince. Jones can't hold back from lampooning the things that aggravate him in contemporary society, and while many readers will sympathise with his frustrations, this doesn't quite work in a novel set in the future: we are constantly pulled back to our twentieth-century vantage point. Numerous narrative glitches contribute to this sense of unreality. For example, why should we believe that the characters are 'starving to death' when, only two pages earlier, we're told that Mari feeds the pork stew to the dogs because having eaten it for two days, she's now 'sick of the stuff'?

In essence, *Water* is a parable, shot through with religious symbolism and references to legends and mythologies, drawing in particular on the Judaeo-Christian account of fallen man. Undoubtedly there are moments of pathos here, but often it feels a little heavy handed. Jones tends to spell things out in case we've missed the point. He tells us that 'nature seemed to be exacting revenge on mankind for the harm done over centuries,' and that 'man believed he was a god who could do what he willed with the living world.'

While many would agree with this analysis, the author's voice can feel intrusive; he leaves us little space to come to our own conclusions. By contrast, Cormac McCarthy's post-apocalyptic novel, *The Road,* is one of omissions and ambiguity; despite the powerful biblical resonances, it lacks moral judgement, allowing for diverse interpretations. Proselytising rarely works in fiction – it can leave the reader feeling disengaged, deadened – and *Water* might be perceived as a claustrophobic read in more than one sense.

Jones should be applauded, however, for tackling a hugely difficult subject: we urgently need novelists to explore the problems of climate change within a Welsh context. But he doesn't play to his own strengths here. In a recent interview with *New Welsh Review (newwelshreview.com//article.php?id=561#pagetop)*, the author said that he'd written this book for a readership interested in the 'Standard English Novel', departing from his usual form to please a perceived market. This seems a shame. Let's hope he now returns to the more experimental, less easily defined narratives for which he is celebrated.

***Angharad Penrhyn Jones** lives in Machynlleth, where she works as a freelance writer. She is co-editor of an anthology on female activism,* Here We Stand, Women Changing the World, *reviewed in an NWR podcast, see p39. She has written for many publications, including the* Guardian *and* New Internationalist, *and is currently completing a novel, an extract of which appeared in issue 92 of* New Welsh Review.

Winter Moorings Andrew McNeillie

Carcanet, £9.95, PB, ISBN 9781847772480

Vicky MacKenzie applauds a poet dedicated to land- and sea-scape, climate and ecosystem

Andrew McNeillie is founder of Clutag Press and literary magazine *Archipelago*, one of the finest small press magazines to appear in recent years. He is also Professor of English at the University of Exeter where he set up the MA in Writing, Nature and Place, a course which captures his presiding passions. *Winter Moorings*, McNeillie's sixth collection, is flooded with imagery of the sea, but the real subject matter is time passing, memory and loss. Indeed, surveying the titles of McNeillie's previous collections it's evident that these themes are a constant inspiration: *Nevermore* (2000), *Now, Then* (2002), *Slower* (2006), *In Mortal Memory* (2009) and *Losers Keepers* (2011).

'Place' is a trendy word these days, but McNeillie's dedication to landscape, seascape, weather, ecosystem, rock formation and climate, is a sincere and all-pervading part of who he is and how he lives his life (if one can judge such things from poetry). A keystone poem in his new collection, 'By Ferry, Foot, and Fate: A Tour in the Hebrides', consists of eight pages of loosely rhymed couplets describing a journey via the islands of Barra, the Uists and Skye, to Raasay, which nestles between Skye and the Scottish mainland. Raasay is the focus of Gaelic poet Sorley MacLean's 'Hallaig', which memorialises the clearing of crofting tenants. McNeillie's poem is in part a homage to 'Hallaig' and echoes MacLean's famous image of trees as the ghosts of the evicted residents. MacLean's poem is also a meditation on the passing of time, and begins with a self-penned epigraph, 'Time, the deer, is in the wood of Hallaig'. McNeillie's poem is rich with MacLean's imagery:

> *[...]   the silver-birch trees*
> *All past child-bearing. And hidden somewhere,*
> *Stock still with timeless stare, the deer.*

But there's more to this poem than just homage to MacLean. It's a celebration of island communities, of the unreliability of the ferry, of the sea and sea birds, of black pudding, whisky, Gaelic, the Post Office bus, and the certainty that in the end, 'spring will come, and the ferry.'

McNeillie brings a keen eye for and a patient knowledge of the natural world, always alert to the fellow creatures with whom he shares his much-valued places. In 'Port Sheánia Revisited', he writes: 'Curlew and oystercatcher compare notes / On a scale of limpidity beyond reckoning. // […] // This goes on all day, all night, without human agency. / Why should that not console me?' This isn't to suggest indifference to human life but the opposite: human life means so much (and hurts so much) that he needs the consolation offered by the natural world, and who are we to deny him?

There are frequent touches of wit in McNeillie's poetry – in 'By Ferry, Foot and Fate' he includes the following couplet: 'I'm MacNeice across the Minch of time / But upside down (and less adept at rhyme).' In the same poem he rhymes 'home' with 'half-rhyme', a poet's joke if ever there was one.

McNeillie often reflects on the nature of poetry itself, and its role as a way of making and remembering. He loves to pun, as in 'Strong Lines', in which he writes: 'I spend my days ashore making and mending / Memory into strong lines hooked on rhyming.' In the final poem, 'At the Landfill Site', he's directed to a section 'Reserved for books and manuscripts'. He sees a ghost who mouths at him: 'The journey from darkness into darkness….' This is reminiscent of Bede's sparrow, his metaphor for the life of man, dashing in one door to escape a winter storm, only to fly out another, its moment of light all too brief. Yet despite the darkness, and despite the 'waste' of endlessly recycled words, McNeillie's final word is one of continuation: 'I filled my notebook with another poem.'

Poetry seems to offer McNeillie both hope and consolation. In 'Blind', another pun-riddled poem, he writes of: 'The timeless yarn of the blind: / Not a line but a net of lines. // Consigning oblivion to oblivion.' Great poets have claimed their work can immortalise those remembered in their words. McNeillie makes no such claim, but in 'On Looking into an Old Photograph', he asks, 'Will I ever see you again, my love?' The answer is suggested by the final lines:

> *[…] I steer between travel deferred*
> *And the pleasure of deferral,*
> *Changing down to first from third,*
> *To all but a halt on time's hill.*

Poetry can't cheat time, but perhaps it can slow it down a little.

Whilst most of the poems here can be described as elegiac, an elegy is about celebration as well as mourning. To remember, to mark the passing of something or someone, is to value them. In this collection McNeillie records his love for places and people, and his grief that all things must be lost.

Vicky MacKenzie *lives on the east coast of Scotland and is writing a novel about John Ruskin.*

Mapping the Roads Mike Parker

The AA, £25, HB, ISBN 9780749574352

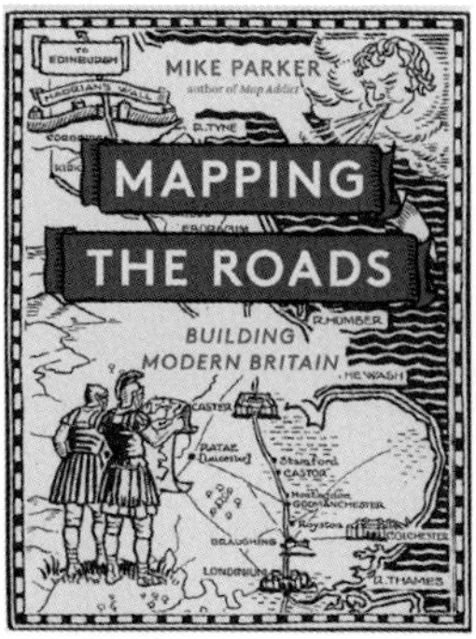

Kat Dawes enjoys a delightful world of tarmacadam, Belisha beacons and thatched petrol pumps

Over 250 pages of gorgeous maps and accompanying text chart the story of Britain's roads, which is also 'the story of our political, economic and social history.' The text is exhaustive, each map the result of huge amounts of work on the part of mapmakers from Roman times to the current definitive Ordnance Survey sheets.

Mapping the Roads is structured chronologically, and the maps in the first two chapters (pre-cars) are gorgeous, often completely baffling, and you could spend many hours poring over them without deciphering what you're looking at. The first is Matthew Paris' thirteenth-century map, which makes Britain look like a lump of dough with blue cracks, carefully labelled with Roman names.

The maps of London are some of the most recognisable. These beauties invite holding the book up to your nose in order to seek out a favourite landmark or street. John Norden's 1593 map of London was the first to use an index at the bottom, and the local guilds' coats of arms are lovingly inscribed on the borders. John Cary's a few pages later shows the fields around Paddington, and Hampstead as a little village entirely cut off from London.

For us in Wales, there is much to enjoy. Many early maps had quite a good grasp of the country, because of our links to Ireland. Thomas Telford's Menai Bridge is carefully described, and there are quite a few lavish maps of our country printed large size. There is a beautiful one from 1873 which would still be of use today which shows the Llyn Peninsula and much of Anglesey.

The prominent mapmakers of each period are presented and many come across as real characters, for example John Ogilby, who started out a destitute boy with his father in a debtor's prison. He ended up winning a lottery and becoming a favourite dancer at court before becoming a publisher, surveyor and mapmaker.

I was tickled to hear where the word 'tarmacadam' came from: John MacAdam built roads of 'crushed stone under a drainable surface' which reduced journey times considerably, and once someone spotted that a barrel of spilt tar also solved the awful dust problem, tarmacadam was born. I'll leave the wry tale of the Belisha beacon for readers to discover....

Later chapters discuss the explosion of road-building and map-making as the bicycle and car appeared and tourism took off. At first it's all Toad of Toad Hall characters blasting about in their expensive cars covering people in clouds of dust and shouting for the speed limits to be removed. Some loved cars, some hated them. A toll road built by the Vanderbilt family in New York allowed drivers to pay $2 then go as fast as they liked; around the same time (1900) the *Financial Times* bemoaned the 'hideous, noisome and noisy vehicles, dangerous alike to wayfarers and to the passengers.' The roadhouses of the 30s grew up when motoring was cool and, with prohibition, the drink-drive rules non-existent. They sound like resorts, offering dance-halls and golf courses, a lot more fun than today's 'get-in, get-out' service stations. Attempts to prettify some roadside garages in the 30s included thatched roofs on petrol pumps — a ridiculous-looking idea.

As motorway building went crazy, voices began to be raised about the decimation of the countryside, and roads gradually became less a symbol of progress and more a site of protest. When things calmed down, politicians began to talk about public transport and reducing road building, all of which is reflected in the maps of the time.

But there's still some fun left too — for example, the 1997 *Upside Down Map* for easing map-reading, conceived by a man but apparently bought mostly by women. For those of us less enamoured with sat-nav, there are a few inevitable tales of lorries stuck under medieval gatehouses and at the edge of cliffs 'as drivers preferred to trust a gizmo from Halfords over the evidence of their own two eyes,' not to mention 'the requisite numpties' heading up Snowdon in flipflops armed with their sat-nav.

This is a behemoth of a book; a leisure drive on a winding coastal highway, not an M25 heart-attack commute. The scope is huge, as befits the impact of the road on our small island. I think anyone who has ever got sidetracked meandering around a map, when supposedly tracking a route, will enjoy this book. Map reading is a very different kind of reading, but it can be equally as pleasurable.

Kat Dawes *is completing a PhD in Creative Writing at Aberystwyth University.*

Marlford Jacqueline Yallop

Atlantic Books, £12.99, PB, ISBN 9780857891051

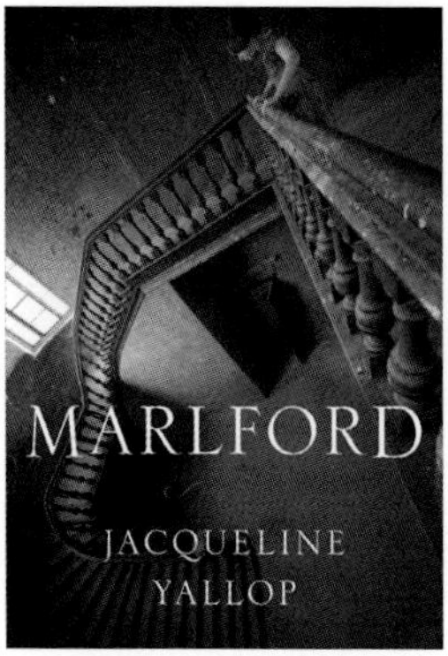

Stevie Davies considers Wales' second Gothic fable of the Big House published by a woman this year

Imagine that, somewhere in England, there existed in the hot summer of 1976 an archaic country house and estate, set up by a bygone philanthropist according to a neo-feudal design. Marlford is owned and administered by the philanthropist's son, Ernest Barton. Decrepitude prevails. The crumbling buildings are undergoing subsidence from abandoned salt mines; the codes that founded Marlford are moribund.

'Every morning during the bleached summer of 1976, when the drought hard-baked the earth, deep down, so that it held still, Ellie Barton went to the mere.' The summer of 1976 has become a legend, mythologised in, for instance, Maggie O'Farrell's *Instructions for a Heatwave*, William Boyd's *Restless* and Deborah Moggach's *Close to Home*. Yallop's prose in the prelude has a lyricism that adeptly captures drought and stillness, life's withdrawal to its base. The mere is a figure for memory. Whatever crime haunts the mere threatens to manifest: 'debris, the accumulated litter of unremembered moments.'

This crime has been committed to secure a future for Marlford's deviant and tottering world: the survival of the estate is predicated on patrilinear inheritance and female infanticide. The single daughter surviving to adulthood is motherless Ellie, centre of Jacqueline Yallop's Gothic fable.

The body of the story occurs in 1969, in the wake of the Summer of Love. Ellie inhabits a stale world where the outlived mores practised by her father are policed by a grotesque team of ageing retainers, Luden, Hindy and Ata, remnants (we later learn) of a First World War POW camp, their names being derived from an earlier generation of European leaders, Hindenburg, Ludendorff and Atatürk. Marlford sidles forward, facing backwards. It's on a hiding to nothing. The retainers are loquacious and rhetorical, speaking a peculiar vernacular: they rule the roost. '"Miss Barton." Luden was stern. "You know what we expect of you, of the mistress of Marlford."'

At Marlford Library there are no, or few, readers. The librarian, Oscar Quersley, tutors Ellie in recondite literature and doubles as a frog-scarer. Ernest Barton, having drowned the babies, or been a party thereto, cannot stand the croaking of the frogs at night. They seem to him, perhaps, to voice the outrage of the drowned girl-babies. What more logical, then, than to post a sentry to silence the frogs?

By now it will be apparent that Yallop's tale is a very peculiar one indeed. Everything is skewed, at a perverse angle to modernity. Ellie lives in a kind of reverie or fugue-state, knowing precious little of the outside world, tied to her duties as the clueless centre of a solipsistic system. Identity is permanently elsewhere: 'But in the avenue behind her, she knew, another girl remained, not quite out of reach, leading some other life.' Marlford's norms deny and defy time, secluded from the world of industry and modernity. There is no electricity. And no radio or television. No newspapers. The clocks are set to a different age. Ellie uneasily inhabits this antechamber to life, until two hippies pitch up, out of the blue, in a van. Now the plot is set in motion and Ellie's education begins.

A man, the hippies tell her, has landed on the moon. 'This is... something has happened? This man, this Mr Armstrong, has landed on the moon? [...] is that right? [...] A man has walked on the moon. And you've kept this from me? Something of this – magnitude?' This quotation exemplifies the oddity of Marlford's various vernaculars. Speech is often precious, wooden or confected. The hippies, Dan and Gadiel, bring, of course, explosive charges – Marxism, civil rights, squatting, sexuality.

The conceit that governs the plot, that of a twentieth-century community cut off from all communication with the world, is frankly preposterous. I didn't believe a word of it. That, of course, need not necessarily matter. In fable or fantasy, the rules of the game may be outrageous but, as long as they are consistent and either entertaining or meaningful, the reader gladly suspends disbelief. Yallop's earlier novel, *Obedience*, also treated the break-up of a closed community. Three nuns, the last of their order, have lived cloistered in a convent – Sister Bernard for over seventy years – protected both from current and past events: they emerge into an altered world but also one that activates memory. *Marlford*'s plot is a less successful fable, on the archaic theme of the strange death of gentry England, with its laws of succession, the role of women as chattel and breeding-stock. The novel is a work of artifice and aestheticism – a literary version of a model village – presenting a carefully crafted, intricately imagined and essentially far-fetched 'What if?'

Stevie Davies *is a novelist and Professor of Creative Writing at Swansea University. She is a Fellow of the Royal Society of Literature and a Fellow of the Welsh Academy; her twelfth novel,* Awakening *(Parthian), was published in 2013.*

Talking to Ourselves Andrés Neuman (trans Nick Caistor & Lorenza Garcia)

Pushkin Press, £8.99, PB, ISBN 9781782270553

Michael Nott loves this novel on illness, grief, sex and literature by a Foreign Fiction Prize nominated team

Talking to Ourselves, Andrés Neuman's second book to be translated into English – exquisitely, in fact, by Nick Caistor and Lorenza Garcia – is both an intimate meditation on mortality and bereavement and an ambitious and intricate narrative collage. It is, in short, an impressive achievement.

At first the premise of the novel seems straightforward – the terminally ill Mario, his wife Elena, and their ten-year-old son Lito, in turns narrate their perspective of the events preceding Mario's death: centrally, the road-trip on which Mario takes Lito through an ambiguous and mystical Latin American landscape. Each narrative takes a different format: Elena, whose frank voice comes to dominate the novel, writes in the form of a diary, the later entries addressed to the deceased Mario, an idea she encounters in her reading of letters sent between Anton Chekhov and Olga Knipper. Of their correspondence, she writes, 'And toward the end, suddenly, like an improvisation amid an empty stage, [Olga] starts to write to her deceased husband. "So, as I write," she says to herself, she says to him, "I feel you are awaiting my letter."'

> *If death interrupts all dialogues, it is only natural to write posthumous letters. Letters to the one who isn't there. Because he isn't. So that he is. Maybe this is what all writing is.*

Elena quotes from, and engages with, a remarkable amount of books – from Geoffrey Gorer to Irène Némirovsky, Javier Marías to Virginia Woolf – each of which seems to help her come to terms with, and make sense of, her situation. Just as she turns to literature to assuage her fragility, she simultaneously becomes involved in an affair with Mario's doctor, Ezequiel Escalante, a dalliance which initially thrills and titillates but comes, eventually, to seem shameful and even disgusting. Elena relates the affair brutally, often in excruciating detail, and Neuman's unflinching prose captures Elena's psychodrama in such a way that we remain empathetic to her disquieting situation.

Mario, in turn, speaks into a tape-recorder, leaving a series of messages for Lito to listen to when he is older, a reversal of Elena's posthumous letters that will never be read. His voice snakes breathlessly through long sentences, each of which, we feel, might be his last. For Elena and Mario, the events of the roadtrip feature only infrequently in their narratives; it is left to Lito to recount such details and events, in his wonderfully digressive, impulsive, and boundlessly energetic stream-like mode of expression. Indeed, Lito is unaware of how ill his father is, and his account becomes increasingly harder to read the more we learn from both Elena and Mario. Neuman pitches the energies of these interspersed accounts beautifully, in particular the similarity in style between father and son.

The drama, then, is not in the inevitability of Mario's death but in how the three voices interrelate. As Neuman's title implies, while their narratives are often addressed to each other, the characters talk mostly to themselves, sometimes in desperation but also for reasons of resistance and solace. This is most evident in their inability to communicate well with each other, and their reluctance to reveal any more than they think necessary, especially relating to Lito. It is, therefore, enormously moving when Mario gives Lito a Lewis Valentino watch at the end of their journey – the gift of time Mario himself is no longer able to give his son.

Talking to Ourselves is a tale exquisitely told, at turns humorous, provocative, and deeply unsettling. Neuman's dexterity in conjuring three persuasive and fascinating characters with voices as unique as you are likely to find in contemporary fiction marks him out as one of the most promising and engaging novelists writing today.

***Michael Nott** graduated from University College London in 2011 with a first-class BA in English Literature. The following year, he graduated with a Masters of Research degree in Creative Writing from the University of Strathclyde, where he worked with the acclaimed novelist, memoirist, and poet Kapka Kassabova. He is now studying for a PhD at St Andrews on the history of photo-poetry.*

The Time Regulation Institute Ahmet Hamdi Tanpınar (trans Maureen Freely & Alexander Dawe)

Penguin Classics, £10.99, PB, ISBN 9780141195759

Caroline Stockford presents Turkey's Proust and his timely novel of bureaucracy, misplaced progress and lost time

This Turkish novel of 1962 is much more than a highly comical portrayal of bureaucracy and modernisation. On almost every page it places the circus that supports social status under the microscope, reflecting on what is true success and how truthfully we perceive ourselves and others.

Protagonist Hayri Îrdal, a self-confessed failure and horologist, commences writing his memoirs in order to celebrate the recently deceased Halit Ayarcı (Eternal Regulator), a businessman of great charm 'who saw both his future and his past through the prism of the present'. Ayarcı, it seems, could light up any apparently hopeless situation with the rays of his unwavering belief in the positive. Ayarcı takes a shine to Îrdal over a much-lubricated dinner at which they discuss the damage caused to the economy by the modern problem of inaccurate watches. The answer, declares Îrdal, is to regulate time precisely: to establish a Time Regulation Institute with Regulation Stations around Istanbul and a system of fines for those with especially unpunctual timepieces. His idea is inspired by his earlier apprenticeship to Nuri Efendi, clockmaker and producer of handmade almanacs. Nuri Efendi's sayings end up being circulated on flyers distributed all over Istanbul. The technique of reflecting back on life with Nuri Efendi and Halit Ayarcı, Îrdal's 'saintly' benefactor, and the introduction of a calvacade of characters can, ironically, result in readers losing track of time.

Tanpınar here satirises the modernisation that was so uncompromisingly introduced by Atatürk in the 1920s and 1930s and appears to mourn the old Istanbul of fezzes, Eastern dress and highly artistic poetry incorporating words of Persian and Arabic origin that had been banned in 1928. The author was originally a symbolist poet and student of the highly regarded Ottoman Divan poet, Yahya Kemal Beyatlı. This formal emphasis, combined with his persistence in using Arabic and Persian, saw his work languishing in his own country until the 1980s.

This translation is sharp, skilful and smooth in register. Contrary to

English, Turkish sentences run in a grammatical sequence of subject, object, verb, sending the reader's attention along a white-water ride of clauses, held in suspense often for a paragraph in length until finally the verb, with its own cascade of suffixes indicating amongst other things case, tense and person eventually resolves what is happening to whom and when. Such clauses here have been preserved and handled masterfully.

The novel's backbone, its humour, has been deftly transferred. The self-deprecating protagonist is constantly passing judgement on the array of characters that populate his life and attempting, often in contradiction, to distinguish others' perception from true success. Another example of the same theme is opium dabbler Seyit Lutfullah, who sleeps in a ruin, 'Imagine the lead actor in a fantastical play who – still wearing his costume and cloaked in his assumed personality – springs off the stage to continue his performance in the city streets.'

A towering personality to rival Halit Ayarcı is Hayri's rich matriarchal aunt, 'Weighed down as she was with this vast inheritance, my aunt couldn't think of dying without recalling that she would be dying for our sake.' Awakening from a coma, she sits up in her coffin as she is being lowered into the ground to see that she had been given a pauper's funeral whilst her brother and nephew take possession of her worldly goods. 'With half her body jutting out of the casket', she demands to proceed home just as she was borne to the cemetery. 'The bizarre return from the world beyond, the fantastical death of my aunt, now alive in her coffin and nibbling on her savoury bun attracted much attention in the back streets... so that by the time they reached home [she] had entered as a bride... the procession had taken on the aura of a victory march.'

Tanpınar, often compared with Proust, is regarded as the father of the Turkish novel. Nobel Prize winner Orhan Pamuk regards Tanpınar as 'undoubtedly the most remarkable author in modern Turkish Literature.' Like Pamuk, Tanpınar writes about Istanbul with *hüzün*, a word that does not translate into English and is very close to the Welsh *hiraeth*, in this case in terms of time lost rather than past place (which is often the case in Wales).

As under fifty works of literary fiction have been translated into English from the last 500 years of Turkish literary production, this novel presents non-Turkish readers with an unmissable opportunity. In Istanbul, shopping malls and themed venues, such as shipping-container restaurants, are popping up daily. Turkey is a country where, currently, money muffles all calls for reason. Tanpinar's observations, made in 1962, on the absurdities of Westernisation, business and progress are sadly very timely indeed.

Caroline Stockford *holds an MA from the School of Oriental and African Studies, London University, in the History of the Turkish Language and is a translator of Turkish literature and poetry. She lives in Aberystwyth with her two sons and is reading a second MA, in Creative Writing, at Aberystwyth University. A selection of her translations can be viewed at Word Prism, estoniacordfrock.wordpress.com*

Taking Mesopotamia Jenny Lewis

Carcanet Press, £9.95, PB, ISBN 978190618 811 5

The Story of Gilgamesh Yiyun Li

Pushkin Children's Press, £14.99, HB, ISBN 9781782690238

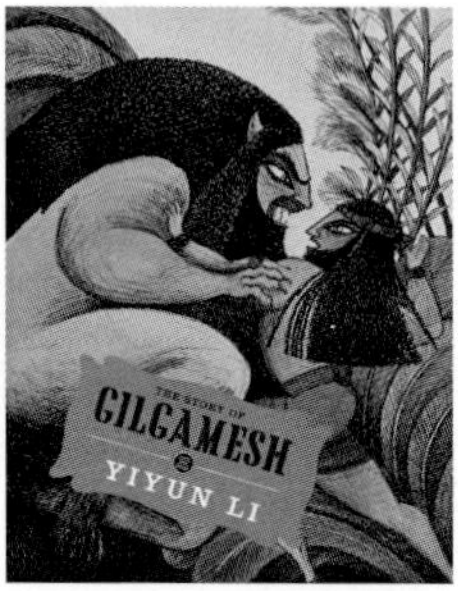

Jane Fraser assesses two books inspired by the Epic of Gilgamesh

These books mesh in theme if not in audience, and are united by themes of hubris and empire-building. Yiyun Li's narrative is aimed to be shared with children by adults, while Lewis' song-like hybrid collection of poetry and prose-poetry is aimed at adults. Both have the Sumerian Epic of Gilgamesh, the oldest piece of written literature in the world, (circa 2,700 BC) as their cohesive glue.

Li has taken the ancient epic (written in cuneiform text on clay tablets in Mesopotamia where it lay undiscovered until brought to light at the end of the nineteenth century) and brought it to life. In this imaginative retelling, her highly acclaimed voice (she has been named by the *New Yorker* as one of the best US writers under forty) directly addresses children of today. Such is the importance of the messages inscribed in the original epic and in her twenty-first century take on it, that Li makes a plea to her young readers to ensure these stories never die: 'One day, when you are old enough, would you do me a favour and tell this story to your children?'

This story, like others in the Save the Story series launched in 2013 by Pushkin's children's imprint, is a 'mission in book form' to save great stories from oblivion by retelling them for a new generation. Production standards match this mission and mean money well spent: quality paper stock, coloured text and stylish, full colour illustrations by Marco Lorenzetti. Here is a beautiful example of the physical presence of print shouting loud and clear it is still alive.

This epic has affected musicians, artists and dramatists down the ages, among whom Lewis herself has stated in interviews that she is 'obsessed' with it and has previously performed *After Gilgamesh* as a play for verse. So what's so special about it? Main character is called Gilgamesh: born to be king – part god, part man, you could say an ancient Mesopotamian superhero, spoilt rotten, toy and tantrum thrower, big ego and big ambitions. A tyrant with an insatiable appetite for power. You could call him Gilgamesh, or by the names of more modern-day tyrants, perhaps Saddam Hussein, George Bush or Tony Blair. But of course, neither Li nor Lewis overtly mentions these names in their work. Li simply says:

> *He occasionally felt something wild and unruly expanding in his heart, which made him hungry for more and more and more. But more what? He did not know... he took small boys from their fathers and threw them around like a child throws his toy robots. This hurt the children, but their crying and screaming only made Gilgamesh bolder and crueller.*

As in all great stories, spoilt brats usually get their comeuppance and emerge changed and wiser. But first there are the usual quests and adventures, a friend (Enkidu) found and lost along the way, love and loss, pain and grief, before a coming to terms with the fact that we face the inevitability of death, even the most elevated and special among us.

Li in her straightforward chronological retelling of often very adult and horrific themes such as rape, violence and death, keeps the context of the original. Place: Uruk, Mesopotamia; time: distant past. Lewis, meanwhile, threads through fragments of the original epic to create a lyrical collection of poetry, witness statements, interviews, diary entries and reports that have been meticulously researched, punctuated with quotes and references back to the original clay tablets on which Gilgamesh was written. Time seems to change nothing in this blood-soaked land, the cradle of civilisation.

Thus the ever-present past and place flow like the ever-constant rivers, Tigris and Euphrates, through the more modern but equally futile landscapes that Lewis juxtaposes. The poet draws parallels (by *showing* rather than Li's *telling*) between the ill-fated and under-funded 1916 British campaign to hold the oil line in Mesopotamia – 'We built a bridge of boats / to reach the so-called Garden of Eden' ('Tom') – and the ill-fated US/UK invasion of Iraq in 2003 – 'Quran, / our birthplace, was a conflagration where Saddam / ruled, Adam and Eve sinned and Alexander died' ('Maryam'). Tom is Jenny Lewis' father, Second Lieutenant Thomas Charles Lewis, who, following his commission by the South Wales Borderers (SWB), was sent with the 4th Battalion to Mesopotamia (Iraq) in 1916. Later, in 1917, he was injured and invalided out to India for eighteen months to recuperate.

> *My face is made from yours –*
> *your jaw, your weak right eye:*
> *my shin bone's from your leg,*
> *shattered in the moonlight....*

Tom later trained as a doctor and married, only to die of a coronary thrombosis when the poet was a few months old. Lewis states in the preface that she has 'been searching for him ever since'. *Taking Mesopotamia* began with research into her father's part in that campaign: the diary-poem 'Tom' is based on factual content in his diaries. It also includes, published for the first time, many of the sixty black and white photographs Lieutenant Lewis took with his Box Brownie camera. Maryam, meanwhile, is a Christian Iraqi, whose interview with the *Guardian* in 2009 inspired Lewis' interview-style poem. This format of juxtapostion of time and place, *them* and *us*, is integral to the successful structuring of the collection.

Lewis gives voice to her own sentiments, but also gives voice to the *other:* those who might not have a voice – past and present. Her anger is controlled, beneath the surface, affecting the reader powerfully with her stance on war as a torrid affair. Also impressive is the poet's commitment to building bridges between international communities, represented by the translation into Arabic of eleven of her poems. Her message of collaboration it would seem is not lost in translation, but is to be shared on stages throughout the world. For Lewis there is no *other* and she is 'mindful of the fact, that in another era, the young men killed and wounded could have included my own two sons, Tom and Edward.' They might also have included Maryam's son, in Qurna, or the sons of Uruk in 2,700 BC.

Both these books tell of quests too: Li's version is of Gilgamesh's ultimate quest for immortality and his hubris before accepting his own mortality. Lewis' is both a personal quest to find the father she never knew (I don't know whether she finds resolution) and an exploration of the tragedy of war. She is also on a bigger quest for peace among nations. Lewis will take many on that search with her, such is the overwhelming poignancy of the work, which is testimony that there is a place for poetry in politics. Both books are also united by the perspective of women – mothers, daughters – who see the absurd waste of war. As the original Epic of Gilgamesh Tablet 111 concludes: 'As for humans, their days are numbered, / whatever they do is like a puff of wind.'

Jane Fraser *is a published writer specialising in the short story, poetry and haibun. She has an MA in Creative Writing from Swansea University and is now studying there for a PhD. janefraserwriter.com*

Rhys Davies: A Writer's Life Meic Stephens
Parthian, £20, HB, ISBN 9781908946713

In this category winner at the Book of the Year, **Harri Roberts** observes that in death as in life, Rhys Davies continues to evade the snares of definition

As his biographer points out, Rhys Davies (1901–78) has been a much-neglected writer. Prior to 1996, for instance, the only example of his work still in print was one modest short story collection. The years since have been kinder, with the three-volume publication of Davies' *Collected Stories* (1996–98) making his vast oeuvre of short stories available again to readers. Interest in the writer has also been stimulated by a new edition of *Print of a Hare's Foot* in 1998, his notoriously unreliable 'autobiography', and his debut novel, *The Withered Root* (2007). There has also been a landmark collection of critical essays, *Decoding the Hare* (2001), also edited by Meic Stephens.

Nevertheless, when one considers Davies' literary achievement in terms of quality and output, he deserves to be much better known. Davies was one of those rare creatures in Welsh literature, a full-time professional writer. During his life, he published some twenty novels, three novellas and one hundred stories, not to mention two plays, two Welsh travelogues and *Print of a Hare's Foot* (1969). His work was praised by contemporary critics and writers in Wales, England and America, and appeared in anthologies alongside literary giants such as Salinger, Nabokov and Evelyn Waugh. Always popular in the USA, Davies remains only one of two Welsh writers to have won a prestigious Edgar Award for crime writing.

Why, then, the posthumous obscurity? Meic Stephens comments, 'A writer's reputation is not made on work alone but in the context of the wider literary world.' The archetypal loner, Davies shunned literary cliques and salons 'and had no talent or taste for self publicity'; his work subsequently fell out of favour within English literary circles. Meanwhile, Davies' long, self-imposed exile from his native Wales, with which he had always had an acutely ambivalent relationship, cut him adrift from the country's cultural and political developments. As Stephens' biography makes clear, Davies' middle-class individualism placed him at odds with a Welsh culture that largely defined itself in collective terms. Consequently, though Davies was one of the first English-language authors to tackle the Welsh industrial experience, his writing resists categorisation in 'industrial' terms and is equally unsuited to straightforward historical and socio-political analysis.

There is nothing straightforward about Davies, in either his life or his writing. A homosexual at a time when homosexual acts were illegal, Davies was necessarily forced to adopt a furtive, double life in which an outward respectability concealed a penchant for fleeting erotic encounters among the gay bars of Soho. This need to conceal his true self became second nature to an intensely private individual who remained a mystery to even his closest friends. It is a need reflected in the oblique and allusive style of his writing, in which references to homosexuality are entirely absent or detectable only in displaced or coded form.

Such an elusive personality presents a peculiar challenge to a biographer, who cannot assume anything Davies wrote is true. *Print of a Hare's Foot*, described by Stephens as 'a tissue of half-truths and evasions', is a case in point. Yet inevitably the absence of other evidence forces Stephens to draw on Davies' unreliable testimony, particularly with regard to the author's younger years. A trip to Germany in the 1920s with fellow author HE Bates and the German-born bookseller Charlie Lahr provides an amusing example of Davies' haphazard relationship with facts. In *Print of a Hare's Foot*, the trip is recorded as taking place in the 1930s (presumably so Davies could add the colourful detail of streets swarming with Brownshirts and Hitler Youth) and includes an amusing and self-deprecating vignette of a visit to a brothel. Needless to say, the details of this visit completely contradict the version of events provided by Lahr, while Bates' memoirs fail to mention a brothel at all.

It is unsurprising, therefore, that the elusive 'hare' occasionally gives his biographer the slip. There are contradictions in Stephens' portrayal of Davies which are never completely resolved, perhaps testifying to the complexity of Davies' personality and his posthumous capacity to elude definition. Davies is described as both 'self-deprecating' and of possessing a 'self-confidence [that] seemed at times to border on arrogance', while Stephens never quite decides whether his subject was rampantly promiscuous or whether, as his brother put it, 'Most of [his] sexual life went on in his head.'

Quibbles aside, the book is a fascinating introduction to Rhys Davies' life – and an entertaining read. There is a quirky, understated humour in Stephens' narrative which helps to leaven the drier details of Davies' life (the account of the time Davies is forced to share a bed with a drunken Dylan Thomas is particularly amusing). Hopefully, this biography will entice more readers to the work of this complex and rewarding writer.

A former student of the then University of Glamorgan, ***Harri Roberts*** *published his doctoral research under the title* Embodying Identity: Representations of the Body in Welsh Literature *(UWP, 2009). Harri currently works as a freelance editor, Welsh translator and writer on the outdoors. The author of a number of walking guides, he has recently ventured into e-publishing with his partner Tracy.*

The Road to En-Dor EH Jones (foreword by Neil Gaiman)

Cromen, £18 (PB), ISBN 9781291766905, From £2.45 (Epub & Mobi),
ISBN 9781909696129, www.cromen.co.uk/en/books/endor.html

Paul Cooper finds that a Turkish-set wartime memoir about trickery and resistance to tyranny still has relevance in the age of Derren Brown

Lieutenant Elias Henry Jones was a Welsh officer in the Indian Army, captured by Ottoman forces during the First World War and interned in the notorious Yozgad prisoner of war camp in Turkey. What happened next might never have been known, had the lieutenant not escaped from the camp and written a memoir, originally published in 1919: *The Road to En-Dor*, which is coming out in a new release nearly one hundred years after it was first published, with a foreword by Neil Gaiman.

The autobiographical tale follows the young EH Jones as he adjusts to life in Yozgad under the eagle-eyed camp commandant and his officious underlings. There the story might have ended, too, had the inmates of the camp not decided to experiment with that most quintessentially Victorian spiritualist pastime – the Ouija board.

Two soldiers hold a glass between them, allowing it to rove between a circle of letters and spell out messages from the netherworld. At first, they get nothing. Then, Jones realises that he might pass the time in the camp a little easier if he begins spelling out messages of his own. Soon, he has all his fellow inmates captivated, waiting to hear what the voices from the dead have to say next. Deprived of all stimulation, 'spooking' becomes their primary outlet for investigation and adventure. As Jones gets more and more experienced at faking the voices of the dead, he finds ever more subtle ways of influencing his fellow inmates, always walking a tightrope between discovery and deepening of the deception.

But Jones' hijinks come to an end when he realises that his newfound skills, in conjunction with the superstitious nature of the Ottoman camp commandant, could lead to more than just idle entertainment: it could bring him a real possibility of escaping Yozgad and returning home.

Though ostensibly true, the tale of *The Road to En-Dor* is told in the 'ripping yarn' style of pre-war Imperial narratives such as *King Solomon's Mines*. All the elements are here: the cunning British man, the credulous foreigners, the daring plan. But somehow *The Road to En-Dor* manages to be something much more compelling than the traditional self-congratulatory fiction of Empire. With its close examination of the mechanics of human gullibility, it cuts much deeper to the heart of human nature.

'For every one who has noticed' the trick, Jones tells us, 'there will be a hundred who did not. In matters of observation the truth is not to be discovered by a show of hands.'

It's observations like these, so modern in sensibility, that form the core of the book. As Jones partners with another inmate, Hill, the pair's schemes get ever more convoluted and daring. Soon they have developed a secret code made up of innocuous questions and signals that allows them to give the illusion of reading each other's minds.

The book is haunted not just by Jones' fictional spook, but by the very real ghosts of the war dead. The hardship and suffering of the prisoners in the camp is always kept in the periphery of the tale. While the snow falls around Yozgad, and we're told that nearly half of all prisoners transferred to the camp die on the journey, the prisoners in the camp continue surviving with resolve and acceptance. At one point, Jones promises the camp commandant that he'll help him to find the buried life savings of a family eradicated during the Armenian genocide. Yozgad, we're told, was once an Armenian village, now emptied of its previous inhabitants and turned into a prison camp. The story is often funny, but at times it's also exceptionally dark – and gets darker as the tale unfolds.

So why is *The Road to En-Dor* still relevant? Perhaps because the advances of the past century have done practically nothing to dampen the effects of superstition in people's minds. The tricks EH Jones managed to pull off with such aplomb against his Turkish captors are still used regularly by mediums and preachers of all religions, and seeing a heist of such complexity and ambition pulled off using only these methods is a fascinating insight into how these kinds of tricks are perpetrated every day. The book is about authoritarianism and belief, as well as about the amazing ability of the human mind not just to be fooled, but to fool itself.

If you want to be fooled, Jones tells us, 'Above all, have faith. It is the faithful believer who gets the most gratifying results.' The same could be said of this book. Is everything Jones tells us true? At points I felt that if he was capable of pulling off even a tenth of the deceptions he claims he did in Yozgad, then he was a man more than capable of pulling off a couple more at the expense of the reader.

But that's not the point. True or not, *The Road to En-Dor* is a book about resistance to tyranny, and the evergreen ability of the human spirit to refresh itself through hardship. While some of Jones' allusions and references will be lost on the average modern audience, and could have done with some judicious editing, what has come out of the new version is a taut and insightful tale that most definitely deserves another turn on the bookshelves.

Paul Cooper *is a writer and journalist from Cardiff. His novel,* River of Ink, *is forthcoming with Bloomsbury.*

The Ghost of Dylan Thomas Ruthven Todd

Happen*Stance*, £3.60 PB, ISBN 9781910131008

The Mythic Death of Dylan Thomas Robert Minhinnick

Happen*Stance*, £2, PB, ISBN 9781905939923

Amy McCauley uncovers pamphlets shedding light on the old myths of Dylan Thomas' life and New York City death

To coincide with the centenary of Dylan Thomas' birth, Happen*Stance* has released two slim pamphlets. One is a memoir by Thomas' friend, Ruthven Todd, the other a short reflective essay by the poet Robert Minhinnick. Each book deals with the aftermath of Thomas' death in New York, and each (in its own way) calls for a reconsideration of the myths surrounding Wales' most (in)famous poet.

The Ghost of Dylan Thomas – written by Todd, a poet and novelist – collects two pieces of memoir. The first is a previously unpublished article held in the National Library of Scotland; the second offers extracts from an article first published in the early nineteen-eighties. Todd, who first met Thomas in 1934, spent time with him in London where, according to Peter Main, they 'roistered together, stole each other's girlfriends, [and] composed scurrilous verse.' In his afterword, Main goes on to say that during Dylan's four trips to America (between 1950 and 1953) they 'met up often in New York's Greenwich Village where Dylan made final revisions to the manuscript of *Under Milk Wood* in the basement of Ruthven's house.' Todd himself says he 'probably knew [Thomas] over a longer period of time than any other person in the literary world in which we both moved.'

These claims to a kind of 'authority' are carefully – and wisely – established, and the first of Todd's articles offers a fascinating first-hand account of the part he played in Thomas' burial. As a piece of history, this strand of memoir is a marvellous read: Todd relays the events with humour and self-awareness. He describes, for instance, consoling John Berryman who was 'in a state of almost total collapse' after hearing of Dylan's death. He also reflects on his own thorny relationship with Thomas, saying: '[h] e was a friend of a rather difficult sort. I knew that he could and would outsmart me on all occasions, but I also knew he would charm me into forgiving him shortly after. I admired his poetry but I was never certain where I stood with him as a person.'

Todd then reflects on his aborted attempt to 'write the official life' of Dylan Thomas – a task given him by the trustees of Dylan's estate. His direct (and quite frankly, humbling) honesty gives the writing a bittersweet verve. Todd says, 'I started collecting material in both England and America, and soon began to realise I wasn't collecting material about the odd little Welshman I had known and liked; I was horribly involved in the creation of a mythology.' His interviews with Thomas' friends and associates eventually filled thirty-eight notebooks which, Todd says, contained 'several hundred different Dylans'. 'I began to think I was going mad,' he writes, 'Dylan had ceased to be a real person and had become a figment in the mind of each individual who had met him.' The 'haunting' of Todd by these mythological Dylans drove him, sadly, to burn his notebooks and have done with it: but I couldn't help wondering what Todd's book might have looked like had he published it. All in all, a fascinating piece of memoir. Full of affection, doubt, and moments of genuine hysteria.

Robert Minhinnick's short essay, *The Mythic Death of Dylan Thomas*, makes the case that 'most people in the UK, and especially I believe in Wales, are interested in Dylan Thomas not because of his poetry, but because he had the good fortune and sound career sense to die a true Bohemian death in New York City.' He states that New York is 'a necropolis for both the fulsomely talented and the prematurely burned-out. In this sense, [Dylan's] death was "mythic".' Minhinnick develops his theory by arguing that if Dylan had died 'in a London hospital two days after, say, a heavy session at the Wheatsheaf or the Fitzrovia, he would be known today, but not celebrated.' That Dylan Thomas died in New York 'was gloriously, crucially romantic to postwar Britain', he writes. 'In 1953, rationing was still going on, eight years after the war. The streets of London and Swansea were pitted with bomb craters. And think of Wales in 1953 – predominantly working class, and thus dangerous to anyone with poetic pretensions in the English language.'

Strong stuff – but persuasively argued. My only problem with the piece is its habit of flitting from topic to topic. Rather than present a structured, methodical argument, Minhinnick's prose seems unable to settle long enough to follow any of his ideas to the end.

This seems a shame given that the ideas are so interesting. Nevertheless, Minhinnick's prose is vigorous and highly readable, and overall this is a thought-provoking pamphlet.

Amy McCauley*'s poetry has appeared widely in magazines, including* Ink Sweat & Tears, New Welsh Review, The North, The Rialto, The Stinging Fly *and* Tears in the Fence. *Her poem, 'Municipal Ambition', appeared in the 2014 Viking anthology,* The Poetry of Sex. *She has recently written a play called* My Baby Girl *and a verse drama based on Sophocles'* Oedipus Tyrannus.

Lighthouses Allison McVety

Smith Doorstop £9.95, PB, ISBN 9781906613891

Claire Pickard is moved by a third poetry collection, inspired by Woolf, where bereavement is a collective emotion

Allison McVety's third collection opens with two epigraphs. The first, from *Mrs Dalloway*, identifies Woolf as a dominant influence on the work. The second, a quotation from French writer Elizabeth Badinter, establishes loss, particularly parental loss, as one of the central themes of the volume.

This sense of loss recurs insistently throughout the collection but appears most strongly in relation to the death of McVety's own parents. What is perhaps most remarkable about these poems is the way in which bereavement is presented, not as a private, but as a collective emotion. In 'Finlandia', the poet's grief for her mother spreads, like the music played by her father. It reaches through her family, to her neighbours, even to her mother's body in the chapel where, for a moment, it achieves a 'remaking' of loss through the image of her mother's 'blue lips / warming, parting, and for a moment / breathing again'. In 'Light House', McVety's dying father mistakes his daughter for his late wife. In these moments, the poet writes, 'I felt I knew love'. Her father's disappointment as he recognises his error is felt almost as a literal weight yet, even at such a moment of estrangement, the collective nature of grief remains: the moment 'was mine / and hers and his to have' and now, after a decade, it becomes the reader's as well.

Woolf's influence is apparent from the start. The second poem in the volume, entitled 'To the Lighthouse', is the axis around which the rest of the collection revolves. This text, with which McVety won the National Poetry Competition, copies the tripartite structure of Woolf's work of the same name. It follows the poet from her initial failure to read the novel for her English 'A' Level to her return to the book after her mother's death. The poem mirrors Woolf's preoccupation with time whilst simultaneously reflecting the passing of time in the poet's own life. From the examination hall where she 'watched / the future show its pulse', McVety moves to the personal understanding that, as Woolf demonstrated, 'everything big happens in parenthesis'.

Subsequent poems in the collection are united by McVety's attempt to explore what 'everything big' might include. Essentially, this is the journey described in 'Hedging' as the passage 'from bud / to grieving'. The scale on which the poet identifies such loss is impressively vast. It encompasses the First World War, a Cornish mining disaster, pandemics, and also individual tragedies such as those of a girl who fell to her death whilst comet-watching in 1910 and of Margaret Larney, sentenced to be executed for filing coins in 1758. Yet McVety never allows the sadness to overwhelm her reader. Instead, she uses loss to throw into relief moments of intense vitality. Thus, an encounter with the dying Nureyev leads us to 'understand breath – / how raw it is, how infinite it makes us feel'.

The final poem, 'Lookout', emphasises the significance of such moments. It is headed by Woolf's remark that 'I meant to write about death, only life came breaking in as usual'. This poem returns us to Woolf's *To the Lighthouse*. It echoes the ending of the novel with its sense of a journey ambiguously completed. In the opening poem of the collection, 'White House', the narrator is positioned as a painter. With hindsight, the reader suspects that this is meant to align the poet with Woolf's character, Lily Briscoe. Lily famously achieves her 'vision' by synthesising disparate elements of the past, and of perception, through her painting. At the end of her collection, McVety, like Lily, has looked backwards, to Woolf's novel, to history and to her own life. Her final vision also revolves around the reconciliation of apparent opposites: 'I'm a wishbone in sight of its wish. / The seagulls are laughing and flying stock still.' McVety's achievement is to make us believe that, although there is tension here, there is also hope.

Claire Pickard *completed a doctorate on literary jacobitism and gender at Oxford in 2006, after which she took an MA in Creative Writing at Bath Spa.*

SKULLS, ROSES AND DYLAN THOMAS

LUCY GOUGH ON ADAPTING *ADVENTURES IN THE SKIN TRADE* FOR THE STAGE

> **The message was about the melodrama and madness of adolescence**

ON A RECENT VISIT TO POUNDLAND, I WAS IRRESISTIBLY DRAWN TO AN ELECTRIC blue mouse mat decorated with blood red roses and luminous white skulls.

As I paid my pound the cash display described the object as a 'teenage boy's mouse mat'. Suddenly the reason why Kurt Cobain and Queen of the Stone Age feature dominantly in my playlist and why skulls and other teenage iconography clutter my study became clear. It also explained why reading *Adventures in the Skin Trade*, Dylan Thomas' unfinished novel, made such an immediate and deep impression and why I was ready and willing to undertake the many challenges of adapting it for the stage.

From the minute I started reading, I connected with its underlying anarchy, rage and rebellion as the nineteen-year-old Samuel Bennett cuts up photos of his family, smashes the family china and stuffs his sister's crochet up the chimney, before leaving Swansea for a new life and adventures in London. I was engaged by its energy and boldness, and instinctively felt sure that Theatr Iolo's brief to find its appeal for a young audience would be possible.

My inner teenage boy knew how to connect to a young audience: embrace the random surreal logic of the stories, avoiding the temptation to rationalise them into a clear logical narrative. The message was about the melodrama and madness of adolescence.

These stories can be read as a metaphor for all the raw, wild and absurd experiences of being young, leaving home, losing virginity, being lost and getting drunk with strangers. Samuel Bennett travels by train, sits in the station buffet, gets his finger stuck in a bottle, visits a house full to the ceiling with furniture and nearly drowns in a bath drinking eau de cologne while being seduced by Polly and watched by parrots. His encounter with Polly in the bathroom as she tries to 'pull the bottle off his finger' encapsulates all of this so wonderfully. Comedy and pathos are there in bath-fulls.

Woven in is Samuel Bennett's aspiration to be a poet and all accompanying pretensions and self doubt. This synergy of a reckless teenage boy and a newly forming poet makes the work utterly believable and engaging. The vivid poetic imaginings of Samuel Bennett are allowed free reign: 'Or will the room be as full as a cemetery, but with the invisible dead breathing and snoring all around you, making love in the cupboards, drunk as tailors in the dry baths?'[1] But this is always brought to heel by the self doubt, fear of pretension, self loathing and revelation of personal details: 'A keeper of ear wax and nail clippings.'[2] To see how I resolved my struggle to bring all these interior workings to the stage, come and see the play.

Thomas' heightened poetic style of writing is a world away from the spare, snappy exchanges of most drama familiar to young contemporary audiences. And yet it captures a reality which this age group will totally buy into. Writing poetry and songs is so often an outlet for young minds and emotions. I've read somewhere that the teenage brain has been shown to have an overdeveloped emotional side compared to its rational counterpart.

And so despite all its craziness, there is an internal logic at work in Thomas' novel, making sense in that profound way of the subconscious mind, one which adolescents will recognise.

Recently, in London, the TV company I was meeting admitted that having read another of my scripts (full of boys in wolf skins running in gangs, a philosophical tattooist and heavy rock music), they expected its author to be a shaven-headed, possibly tattooed young man. Imagine their surprise when I walked in. But I knew I had written this piece with that gritty part of me that helped me adapt *Adventures in the Skin Trade*. I may be a female writer of a certain age but I glimpsed my soul in Poundland.

Lucy Gough *writes for theatre, radio and television. Among her credits are* Hollyoaks *and a version of* Wuthering Heights *for Radio Four's primetime mid-morning slot. She has written a play on the artist and writer Brenda Chamberlain, currently titled* Menaced by Nightingales, *for National Theatre Wales. Her adaptation for Theatr Iolo of Dylan Thomas'* Adventures in the Skin Trade *goes on tour this autumn, theatriolo.com.*

[1] *Adventures in the Skin Trade*, Dylan Thomas, New Directions (1953).
[2] Thomas, op cit.

DISCOVER …

more exclusively online reviews

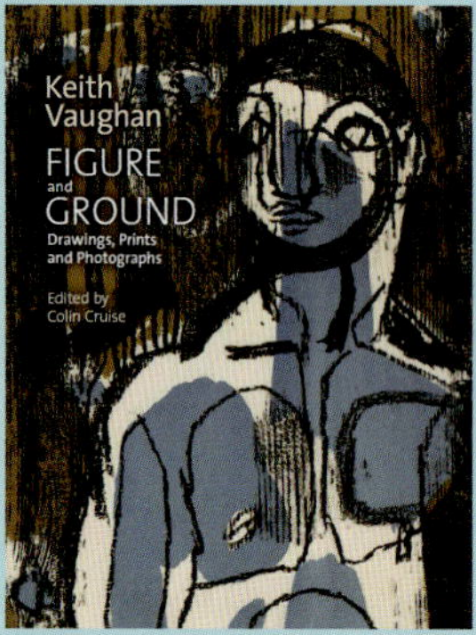

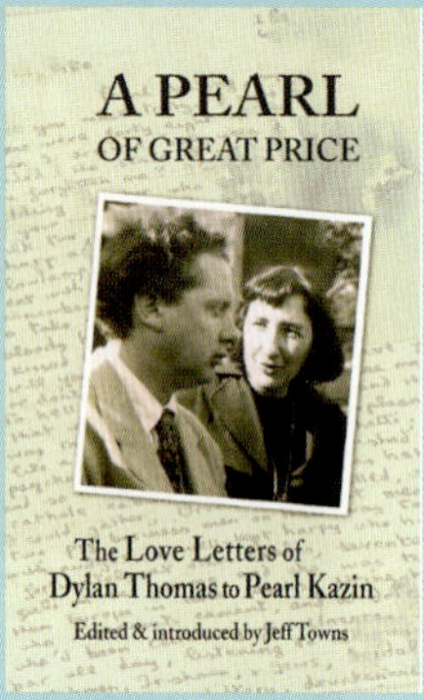

Keith Vaughan, Figure and Ground

Simon Pierse, Harry Heuser, Robert Meyrick; ed Colin Cruise (Sansom)

Amy McCauley admires this book on an overlooked aspect of Keith Vaughan's work on the male form: his photography, prints and draughtsmanship, drawn from a collection held at Aberystwyth University.

Six Pounds Eight Ounces
Rhian Elizabeth (Seren)

For Philip Clement, the voice of Rhian Elizabeth's precocious five-year-old protagonist is beautifully self-assured, coaxing the reader into the growing pains of a girl experimenting with truth, fiction and Tonypandy. Comparisons with Rachel Trezise are inevitable.

A Pearl of Great Price: The Love Letters of Dylan Thomas to Pearl Kazin
ed & intro Jeff Towns (Parthian)

Vicky MacKenzie concludes that while these letters offer some new gems for fans, it's doubtful whether they offer a significant contribution to our understanding of either the work or life of Dylan Thomas.

'Tulips' by Nancy Whistler, courtesy of Jim Pratt.

COMING UP **NWR** WINTER 2014

Literary & early Welsh tourism

Niall Griffiths on St Helena

Borders stories with Nicholas Murray

& Nancy Whistler